T0157479

WHATCHA TALKIN' 'BOUT GOD?

A Simplified Guide to Reading or Studying the Bible

Kathy Lee Rix, MBA, BBA, Ph.D

WESTBOW
PRESS®
A DIVISION OF THOMAS NELSON
& ZONDERVAN

WestBow Press books may be ordered through booksellers or by contacting:

WestBow Press
A Division of Thomas Nelson & Zondervan
1663 Liberty Drive
Bloomington, IN 47403
www.westbowpress.com
844-714-3454

ISBN: 979-8-3850-1131-5 (sc)
ISBN: 979-8-3850-1132-2 (e)

Library of Congress Control Number: 2023920813

Print information available on the last page.

WestBow Press rev. date: 12/14/2023

Dedicated to ...

… my two sisters in Christ, Pamela Robertson, and Laura Shockley. Both of you have invested years encouraging me and guiding me along this path. You rejoiced and praised God with me when I was on the mountain tops; you cried and prayed with me and lifted me up when I was in the valleys. I love you both.

Acknowledgments

I want to thank all of the people who encouraged me and prayed for me during this process. I also want to thank all of the people throughout my life who guided me in God's direction so that I was able to let Him work in me to bring me to this point.

I want to thank those who beta-tested the manuscript and gave invaluable information on ways to improve the document. Much love to Dawn Black, Brandi Coyer, Connie Demske, Al Ritsema, and Sheila Ritsema.

Most of all thank you to my editor, Kaitlin Ives (https://www. writingsosmentor.com), who diligently reviewed each page for both copy and content. Through her prayerful guidance, I was able to elevate this manuscript above what it was before.

Foreword

Kathy Rix's study guide is an incredibly helpful and easy-to-approach guide for anyone looking to grow in their ability to understand and interpret the Bible. Sometimes it can feel daunting as we approach this ancient text with its odd turn of phrase, its unfamiliar historical context, and its sheer size. Where do we start? How do we know that we are understanding it correctly? Kathy's short volume helps the student approach the Bible with confidence.

Kathy is a teacher. Her heart to see people grow and thrive in their lives is evident when you sit down with her. Her passion for the word of God is equally obvious and these qualities combined are clearly seen throughout this volume. You can rest assured that you are in good hands as you dive into *Whatcha Talkin' 'Bout God?*

What I appreciate most about this study guide is how effectively Kathy has laid it out for the beginning student. Anyone from any walk of life could come to this study and learn how to read, study, and apply the Bible. She expertly discusses the big picture of what the Bible is, what the deal is with all these translations, and how the various genres of the Bible need to be read in order to accurately interpret them. These things can be overwhelming, and I was excited to see how approachable she made these topics for readers who are new to the Bible.

But, she also helps those who have been reading the Bible for years and years. What is the difference between reading and studying? How do I interpret what I have always *assumed* that I understood? How do I internalize and apply these things that the Bible is saying? All of these questions and more are answered here.

I am excited to see how this study helps the body of Christ to grow in their understanding and comfort with the Bible. Kathy has synthesized a ton of information that is all here for the Bible student looking to grow their confidence and ability to study the Scriptures. If these ideas are consistently applied, you will see the Word of God transforming you more and more into the image of Christ and you will grow in your effectiveness to fulfill the call that God has put on your life.

Mark Morris
Adult Life Stage Pastor, Centerpoint Church
Kalamazoo, Michigan

Preface

Why This Study Guide?

When you become a new Christian, the first thing everyone says is, "Read the Bible." It is important to understand that Bible study begins with actually reading Scripture not just books about the Bible or devotional materials based on it. That would be like trying to learn how ice cream tastes without actually eating any. You will never get the full flavor of it.

When I first tried to venture into reading and studying the Bible around 30 years ago, the reference materials—the stuff I looked at to find out how—were very complicated. They used big, complicated words that I did not understand. It really discouraged me from moving forward with my reading. I pray that this study guide eliminates that scenario.

While the literature on reading and studying the Bible has gotten better, there are a *lot* of resources out there. I have scoured over 30 resources to gather and synthesize the best information on the topic. I have taken the best and most understandable information from each resource and combined it into this one guide in an effort to answer the questions that most new Christians—or even those who just want to know more about Bible study—might ask. Think of this guide as a glorified FAQ on how to read or study the Bible.

Why You?

You may be asking yourself why you should complete this guide. The answer varies depending on where you are in your walk with the Lord.

YOU'RE NEW TO THE WALK

If you have recently become saved (asked Jesus into your heart and given your life over to Him), reading and studying the Bible can seem overwhelming. You may be wondering where to start. Or how to do it. Or why you should do it. This guide will answer the why and then take you through the steps of how to get started.

YOU'VE BEEN WALKING A WHILE

If you have been walking with Jesus for a while, some of the things covered in this guide will be familiar to you. But, even if it is familiar, this guide will provide you with a more focused process for reading and studying the Bible.

Are you in a position where others might ask you why they should read the Bible? This guide will help you provide them with sound reasons other than, "Because God says so." You will be able to discover good answers for other questions, too. All of this will create an opportunity for you to guide them in getting started.

Why Me?

During my career as an Association Registrar for Operations and Technology at a midwestern university, I was asked to write numerous procedure manuals. The staff members who used those manuals expressed their appreciation for the clarity and conciseness the manuals contained. They said it made learning the new process much less stressful; that they were more successful in learning the process because of the manuals. I have used the same philosophy in creating this guide.

While I have several educational credentials after my name (see list below), the overriding reason I have written this guide is that God has instilled within me a burning passion to help others acquire a closer, deeper, more personal relationship with Jesus. To that end, He has called me, while following His guidance, to write curriculum. This guide is the first of several topics He has laid on my heart. Other study guides will follow.

Educational Credentials
- 1994: BBA in Office Administration
- 1999: MBA in General Management
- 2008: Ph.D. in Higher Education Administration with a focus on serving adult (age 25 or greater) students.
- 2017: Certificate—Wellspring School of the Heart

My Prayer
Lord Jesus, thank You for Your eternal, unconditional love, Your persistent presence, Your all-encompassing grace, and Your gracious mercy. Bless the life of each person who chooses to use this guide. Give each one eyes to see and ears to hear. Fill everyone with Your spirit of Wisdom and let every person's relationship with You grow ever closer and deeper. I ask this in Your Holy name. Amen.

Chapter Layout and Formatting

Chapter Layout

While additional sections are added to some chapters based on the subject matter, each chapter has the same seven sections as its core.

What the Chapter is About

This section will always appear first in the chapter. It is a synopsis of what you will learn in the chapter and why it is important.

Prayer

Beginning each session of study with a prayer is crucial. Think of it as a lesson pre-requisite from God. Therefore, there is a short prayer provided at the beginning of each chapter. Feel free to either read this offering with a prayerful attitude to make it your own, or to create your own prayer. The critical factor is that you ask God for His guidance and illumination as you work through the material.

Chapter Verse

Each chapter verse was prayerfully chosen to reflect the theme of the chapter. If you want to delve deeper after completing the chapter, you could do an in-depth study of this verse.

Coming to Terms with Terms

To minimize distraction, all of the definitions have been placed at the beginning of the chapter. This allows you to familiarize yourself with what the terms mean before you encounter them in your reading. Hopefully, this will make the reading of the text flow more smoothly, which should lead to a fuller understanding of the topic. Conversely, the first time the definition word is encountered in the text it will appear in a *SPECIAL FONT* to remind you that it is defined at the start of the chapter.

Summary

This is a short recap of the pertinent points presented in the chapter. If you get to this point and do not understand something mentioned in the summary, you should go back through the chapter to review and obtain more knowledge on the subject.

Coming Attractions

This is a brief introduction of what the next chapter will cover. It is kind of like the teasers you see at the end of your favorite TV show.

Points to Ponder

Each chapter will have a review of the primary topics covered. It is important to record your answers, not just think of an answer in your head. You can use the space provided in the book or a separate sheet of paper, either handwritten or on a computer. Whatever works for you.

Recording your answers is important for four reasons.

1. It firmly embeds the material in your memory and your spirit.
2. If you are doing the study as part of a small group or in a classroom setting, a review of these points will be part of the session. By recording your responses, you are free to listen to the thoughts of others instead of trying to recall your answers.

3. It allows you to go back at a later date to review the material.
4. By writing your answers, you often will find that you know things you didn't think you knew. Once the words start flowing, God can bring other points into your consciousness.

Just as important as starting your study with a prayer is ending it with one. Therefore, the last instruction in each *Points to Ponder* will be to construct your own prayer, asking God what He wants you to take away from the chapter. This does not need to be a dissertation. It can be as short as a single question, a couple of sentences, or a short paragraph.

Other Formatting Features
There are a few other elements that have been carried throughout the chapters.

Defined Words
The first time you encounter any of the words defined under *Coming to Terms with Terms*, it will appear in a SPECIAL FONT to remind you that it is defined at the start of the chapter.

Citations
Because information from various sources has been highly synthesized, or multiple sources contain the same information, all references for a paragraph appear at the end of the paragraph. Hopefully, this will provide a better flow of information with less breakage in your train of thought as you read.

Quotations
All direct quotes used have been indented and set in their own paragraphs. Many times, after I have read a book, I want to refer back to a quote that was provided. When the quotes are embedded into the text they are hard to find, which can be frustrating. So, I have set them apart.

Wide Margins
This guide was written with the desire that you will devour it and make it your own. Part of that process, in addition to highlighting, is jotting down your own thoughts. In many books, you have to squeeze these into a very small margin. Frustrating, right? Well, plenty of white space has been provided for your own ideas, so jot away.

Contents

Introduction

How Does This Work?

How to Use This Study

PLEASE READ THIS CHAPTER. It is the key to understanding how the study guide works. It contains explanations of the format as well as important tips to help you get more out of your journey.

Prayer

Father God, thank you for instilling in me a hunger to know your Word better. As I work through this study guide, I ask that the Holy Spirit open my spiritual eyes and ears so that I can better receive what You are teaching me. I ask this in the name of Jesus. Amen.

Chapter Verse: *Psalm 14:2*

ESV	*The LORD looks down from heaven on the children of man, to see if there are any who understand, who seek after God.*
NIV	*The LORD looks down from heaven on all mankind to see if there are any who understand, any who seek God.*
NLT	*The LORD looks down from heaven on the entire human race; he looks to see if anyone is truly wise, if anyone seeks God.*

Coming to Terms with Terms

Learning these translation abbreviations would be beneficial, as they are standard throughout literature and the web. The most common are marked with an asterisk (*).

All scriptures in this study were downloaded from either the Blue Letter Bible website (www. blueletterbible.org) or the You Version website (www.bible.com).

*AMP**	Amplified
ASV	American Standard Version
CEB	The Common English Bible
*CSB**	Christian Standard Bible
ESB	English Standard Bible
*ESV**	English Standard Version
GNB	Good News Bible
GNT	Good News Translation
*KJV**	King James Version
*MSG**	The Message (Not an official translation, but often treated as one.)
*NASB**	New American Standard Bible
NCV	The New Century Version
*NIV**	New International Version
*NKJV**	New King James Version

NLT*   New Living Translation

TLB   The Living Bible

Scripture References

Except for the chapter verse, each Scripture presented will be given a reference number for easier notation in the text. These references numbers reset to one (1) at the beginning of each chapter.

Presentation

Because no single Bible translation is *the* translation, each verse will be presented in multiple translations. The primary four used are ESV, CSB, NIV, and NLT. My intent is to give complete, well-rounded information. Therefore, if the verses are almost identical, i.e. they translate all the key words the same, only those translations that enhance the meaning of the verse(s) will be presented.

PLEASE NOTE: The Message (*MSG*) was written without verse numbers. While electronic versions of the Bible often place a few here and there so that the computer can find stuff, the verses in this study that come from the Message paraphrase will not contain verse numbers except in the reference line.

Importance

The Scriptures have been carefully chosen to either support a point or expand your understanding. Please do not skim over them but read them carefully and absorb them into your spirit.

To Help You Get More from the Study Guide

This section is a collection of unrelated hints that can help you get more out of this guide.

Reading vs. Studying

Throughout the guide you will find references to the phrase *reading or studying*. "Why both?" you might ask. It is because they are different activities, approached in separate ways.

READING THE BIBLE is simply that. You read the text, only stopping when you need to refer to a footnote for clarification of something. Usually, when reading, you will cover more ground, maybe several chapters in a sitting. It is a matter of discovering what Scripture says.

STUDYING THE BIBLE goes much deeper. You generally will cover only a few verses in a sitting, rarely more than a chapter. You will use various study tools—discussed in chapter four—to dig deep into what the passage is saying and how it applies to you and your life. It is a matter of discovering what Scripture means, both then and now.

How Do You Learn?

When you know your learning style, you can optimize your study time by using the style(s) that works best for you. If you do not already know your predominant learning style, you can discover it by completing a learning style inventory.

The inventory is not a required part of this study, but, especially if you are still a student, it could be very illuminating and help in future learning endeavors. I have included two different inventories; one is a PDF to be printed (found on the Google drive) and the other is online. The URL for the online version is included in the *URLs for Websites and Supplemental Resources* document found on the Google drive (https://docs.google.com/document/d/1MJE6hhst0xDrOexgzm6upyTf64Tj-PNlhzs3cpo_xLc/copy). Hint: If you choose the online inventory, set the number of questions per page to 50, because, depending on your provider and your internet speed, each page could take several seconds to load. Since there are 70 questions, it limits the number of times you are waiting for the page to load to only two.

Expectations

Whether you are part of a group or completing the study guide on your own, there are certain expectations, or assumptions, that are basic. Please note that a group can be either a small group of about 10-12 maximum (more chance for discussion that includes everyone), or it can be more of a classroom setting, where the leader is presenting the material (probably less opportunity for everyone to share).

The primary assumption, since this is not a required course anywhere, is that you truly have a hunger to know God better as well as to learn how to read or study Scripture better. These goals will be achieved if you seriously consider all content presented and prayerfully read all verses provided. Additional understanding will come from responding—in writing—to the *Points to Ponder* questions at the end of each chapter. If you are unsure of any of the material presented, discussing it with a person who is farther along in their walk with God can help clarify it for you.

The rest of the expectations refer primarily to group study.

DO THE HOMEWORK

You will get the most out of your group sessions if you have studied the chapter prior to coming to group. Because discussion is a large part of the learning curve, the suggested agenda for group meetings (available on the Google drive at https://docs.google.com/document/d/1_3dJUSXehCe_nNQGkQ_-tAeRB0l32cWkG4aKePL9RV8/copy) does ***not*** include reviewing the text. It focuses on discussion of the things learned in the chapter, starting with the *Points to Ponder* and expanding to other topics as the Holy Spirit leads.

RESPECT AND CONFIDENTIALITY

Groups are to be safe places for everyone to learn and grow as well as to express ideas. One very important expectation is that every person who is part of a group will respect the ideas and comments of the other people in the group. If ideas are not in line with Scripture, someone in the group, usually the leader, can gently and lovingly explain why and then give guidance as to what would be a Scriptural response.

Along these lines, everyone is expected to maintain the confidentiality of all the members of the group. Again, this goes toward groups being a safe atmosphere in which people can be ministered to as needed.

Additional Documents

There are several supplemental reference documents for this guide. All are housed on a Google drive, but some are contained in the appendices, also.

The files held on the Google drive require URLs. These are available in a document found both in Appendix A and at https://drive.google.com/file/d/1f8nb23QuIH2_-pq_dzsW9y2YDK3p7KsA/copy.

Use this page for notes.

Use this page for notes.

1

What's in it For Me?

Why Do I Need to Study the Bible?

This chapter explains why it is so important to read and study the Bible. Although by no means an exhaustive list, you will learn the many benefits of reading the Bible. You will see how it can change you and your life as well as how it can affect those around you.

Prayer

Father God, thank you for your enduring love. Thank you for putting the desire in my heart to know you better. Lord Jesus, take the things I will read here and use them to teach me more about You and how to know You better. Holy Spirit, open the eyes and ears of my heart to see and hear what You are saying to me. I realize that what You have to say to me may not come from the words on these pages, but I am eager to hear them anyway. Lord, in the name of Jesus, I ask You to bless this time of study. Amen.

Chapter Verse: 2 *Timothy 3:16-17*

ESV	[16]*All Scripture is breathed out by God and profitable for teaching, for reproof, for correction, and for training in righteousness,* [17]*that the man of God may be complete, equipped for every good work.*
CSB	[16]*All Scripture is inspired by God and is profitable for teaching, for rebuking, for correcting, for training in righteousness,* [17]*so that the man of God may be complete, equipped for every good work.*
NLT	[16]*All Scripture is inspired by God and is useful to teach us what is true and to make us realize what is wrong in our lives. It corrects us when we are wrong and teaches us to do what is right.* [17]*God uses it to prepare and equip his people to do every good work.*

Coming to Terms with Terms

DOCTRINE: A principle or position or the body of principles in a branch of knowledge or system of belief: dogma.

GRAPHÉ: Something written, a document. Used 51 times in the New Testament.

LOGOS: Either written or spoken. Although it can be specific, it usually represents the big picture, such as an idea, topic or motive, or the reasoning behind them. Used 316 times in the New Testament

RHEMA: According to *Thayer's Greek Lexicon,* this is the spoken word of God. Properly, that which is or has been uttered by the living voice, thing spoken, word. Teaching that produces eternal life (see Scripture #1). Utterances in which God, through someone, declares his mind (see Scripture #2). Used 67 times in the New Testament.

Scripture 1: **John 6:68**

CSB	*Simon Peter answered, "Lord, to whom will we go? You have the words of eternal life.*
NLT	*Simon Peter replied, "Lord, to whom would we go? You have the words that give eternal life.*

Scripture 2: **John 8:47**

ESV	Whoever is of God hears the words of God. The reason why you do not hear them is that you are not of God.
CSB	"The one who is from God listens to God's words. This is why you don't listen, because you are not from God."
NIV	Whoever belongs to God hears what God says. The reason you do not hear is that you do not belong to God.
NLT	Anyone who belongs to God listens gladly to the words of God. But you don't listen because you don't belong to God.

Jacket Notes

If you have ever bought a book, you most likely have read the jacket notes before you purchased it. What it is about? What do other people have to say about the book? Now, imagine that the book you are considering is the Bible. From the jacket you learn that the book is about the story of mankind, from creation to residing in heaven. But is it really good? Listen to what others have said.

> The Bible is worth all other books which have ever been printed.
> —*Patrick Henry (Bell & Campbell 2003)*

> The Bible is an inexhaustible fountain of all truths. The existence of the Bible is the greatest blessing which humanity ever experienced.
> —*Immanuel Kant (Bell & Campbell 2003)*

> It is impossible to rightly govern the world without God and the Bible.
> —*George Washington (Bell & Campbell 2003)*

> The New Testament is the very best book that ever was or ever will be known in the world.
> —*Charles Dickens (Bell & Campbell 2003)*

> The Bible is the loving heart of God made visible and plain.
> —*Dallas Willard (Johnson 2003)*

> [The Bible] is not only a book which was once spoken, but a book which is now speaking.
> —*A. W. Tozer (Johnson 2003)*

Those are some pretty good endorsements, right? But wait, there's more good stuff!

You've heard it before, but it's true. God created you for one purpose—to have a relationship with Him, the Triune God. Relationship, by definition, means interaction with each other. God is always there, so it is your task to connect with Him. It is His task to do the perfecting of your life, which He does, partly, through His Word. In John 20:31, God tells you why He gave you His Word (see Scripture 3).

Scripture 3: **John 20:31**

ESV	But these are written so that you may believe that Jesus is the Christ, the Son of God, and that by believing you may have life in his name.
NLT	But these are written so that you may continue to believe that Jesus is the Messiah, the Son of God, and that by believing in him you will have life by the power of his name.

Reading or studying the Bible is a communication with God where you find out who God is. Inhaling these words of life that God carefully breathed on the authors can transform you into a radically different person who thinks as God thinks and loves as God loves. In short, it can transform you into the person God sees when He looks at you. (Barclay [1972] 1997; Johnson 2003)

What the Bible Is and Is Not

The Bible is many things, but at its core it is essentially a revelation of God. It is, in fact, a divine self-disclosure. While the Bible contains scientific facts, it is *not* considered scientific. Likewise, it is *not* literary, it is *not* philosophical, and it is *not* an ordinary book. (ESV Study Bible 2011; Stott 1999)

Graphé, Logos, and Rhema

This author spent the majority of her Christian life differentiating between Logos (as the written word) and Rhema (as the spoken word). However, in a sermon given on December 29, 2019, as well as in a follow-up email on December 31, 2019, Cameron Wright, Pastor of New Day Community Church, opened her eyes to the error of her ways and gave her a whole new point of view that now includes GRAPHÉ.

In Christian references, graphé, LOGOS, and RHEMA refer primarily to various forms of communications from God. While often used interchangeably, they do have subtle differences.

GRAPHÉ is always written and, technically, can refer to any document. However, all of the 51 times it is used in the New Testament it refers to Scripture, either in whole or in part.

RHEMA refers to something spoken or uttered. Technically, everything we say is rhema as the definition of rhema does not limit the words spoken to the word of God. However, in widespread use today, rhema is used to refer to a revelation from God. Always coming through the Holy Spirit, it can happen as a verse or portion of scripture comes to your attention—jumps off the page—that has application to a current situation or need for direction. You would probably recognize it as an *aha* moment.

LOGOS can be either written or spoken. While it can refer to a specific saying, it is a broad, general term that usually represents an idea, thought, reasoning, motive, or the meaning of something.

As it stands when you pick up the Bible, you read the graphé, which can and will turn into rhema that you *hear*. Together they bring an understanding of the logos. As such, the entire Bible can be considered the living word of God. (Advanced Training Institute International 2015; Stott 1999)

Inspiration

The Bible is a God-given guide to us as sinners, but, equally, a handbook that the church can use to guide it in worship and service to God. It is a divinely inspired unity of narrative and associated admonitions or lessons. While activities of God's people before and after His appearance on earth make up its ongoing story, Jesus Christ is the Bible's central focus. He provides the unity. Everything points to Him, His birth, His life, His death and His resurrection. (ESV Study Bible 2011)

Revelation

Don't be misled into a lot of theology. The Bible is much more of a practical book than a theoretical book. The Bible is the place where the Spirit of God and the spirit of man meet in a unique way. This meeting is the first essential basis of any DOCTRINE or revelation. The purpose of God in the Bible is to disclose (reveal) truths about Himself and His kingdom that would have remained unknown and undiscovered if He had not revealed them. Your revelation takes place when God's Graphé becomes God's Rhema. (Barclay [1972] 1997; ESV Study Bible 2011; Stott 1999)

Authority

> There are more sure marks of authenticity in the Bible than in any profane history.
> —*Isaac Newton (Bell & Campbell, 2003)*

The Bible is old. The writings it comes from are even older. Yet, in spite of the antiquity of these writings, they remain trustworthy because of the care and diligence with which they have been transmitted to you, through many people over thousands of years. God still speaks through what He has spoken. You bow to the authority of Scripture because you bow to the authority of Jesus Christ. If you desire to bow to Christ's authority, you also need to bow to Scripture's. It is because of Jesus Christ that Christians submit to both the Old Testament and the New Testament. (Bell & Campbell 2003; Stott 1999)

Difference

While inspiration, revelation, and authority are closely related, they are also distinct. (Stott 1999)

INSPIRATION is the chief mode that God has chosen to reveal Himself to you. He has used it since creation, and He uses it still today. It is His process of communication, although the mode changes (i.e., a vision, spontaneous thought or picture, or verbal—although this is rare).

REVELATION is derived from a Latin word meaning *unveiling*. It indicates that God has taken the initiative to make Himself known. It is when a verse or a truth suddenly makes perfect sense and moves from information in your head to a deep-rooted belief in your heart. It changes from theological truth to your spiritual truth.

AUTHORITY is the power or weight of the Scriptures themselves, strictly because of what they are. They are divine revelations given through divine inspiration. Since they are the Words of God, it has authority over men.

Finding Jesus and God

The supreme importance of the Bible is that in it you find Jesus Christ. There is only one way to gain clear, true, fresh, and lofty views of Him, and that is through the Scripture. Jesus is the grand centerpiece of the entire Bible. Scripture's purpose is to bring you to salvation, and since salvation is through Jesus, all the scriptures point to Him as well as His death and resurrection. (Barclay [1972] 1997; Bell & Campbell 2003; ESV Study Bible 2011; Radiant Church 2015; Stott 1999)

The Bible is the prism through which the light of Jesus Christ is broken into its many beautiful colors. Through it you see love, peace, and forgiveness as well as all the other attributes of Jesus. Additionally, you gain a personal knowledge of God through knowing Jesus. Christians study Scripture because they *know* Jesus, but also because they *want to know* Him more. The Bible is God's own portrait of Jesus, and there is no other way to know Him. (Barclay [1972] 1997; ESV Study Bible 2011; Stott 1999)

Another goal of studying Scripture is to know God. While the Bible reveals Jesus to you, it also gives you God's thoughts about everyday issues of life. The big picture shows how God has interacted with his people throughout history. Reading and studying the Bible is essential for the Christian who wants to know Him on a deeper level. (Bell & Campbell 2003; Johnson 2003; Radiant Church 2015; Stott 2008)

Benefits of Reading

Granted, the Bible is not an easy read meant for a lazy afternoon. So, one logical question might be, "Why bother?" The answer is that the benefits of reading or studying the Bible greatly outweigh the challenges. It can be life changing. God's word is as essential to your spirit for a healthy spiritual life as natural food is to your body for a healthy physical life. The better you understand how to relate to the Bible, the more you can learn to benefit from its teachings. (Bell & Campbell 2003; Stott 1999)

To Grow Your Faith

Both John and Paul present the same sequence of steps to gain salvation: 1) Scripture, 2) Jesus, 3) faith, and 4) salvation. It all starts with the Bible. Its primary usefulness is for you to receive salvation by building your faith through knowing Jesus. (Stott 1999)

Bible knowledge can make you a more spiritual person (see Scripture #4). Every time you read the Bible—and pay attention to what you're reading—you are learning something. Reading the Bible will stretch your mind and expand your thinking. It offers a profound insight into the realm of the unseen (as in the Kingdom of God). It helps you separate truth from mythology, and helps you come to see God less as a tyrant and more as a loving Father, counselor, and friend. As you expose yourself to the biblical witness of this Jesus, and as you feel its impact—profound yet simple, varied yet unanimous—God creates faith within you, you receive the testimony, you believe. (Bell & Campbell 2003; Meyer 2015; Stott 1999)

Scripture 4: **Romans 10:17**

ESV	*So, faith comes from hearing, and hearing through the word of Christ.*
CSB	*So, faith comes from what is heard, and what is heard comes through the message about Christ.*
NIV	*Consequently, faith comes from hearing the message, and the message is heard through the word about Christ.*
NLT	*So, faith comes from hearing, that is, hearing the Good News about Christ.*

To Change Your Life

Studying the Bible, and taking its truths into your spirit, can make you a more virtuous person. If you want to see areas of your life truly transform, learn to study the Bible. It has the power to change you—which alters your life—because there is life in the Word (see Scripture #5). The Bible is a story of rescue. It is meant to transform, not just inform. (Meyer 2015; Radiant Church 2015)

Scripture 5: **Hebrews 4:12**

ESV	*For the word of God is living and active, sharper than any two-edged sword, piercing to the division of soul and of spirit, of joints and of marrow, and discerning the thoughts and intentions of the heart.*
CSB	*For the word of God is living and effective and sharper than any double-edged sword, penetrating as far as the separation of soul and spirit, joints and marrow. It is able to judge the thoughts and intentions of the heart.*
NIV	*For the word of God is alive and active. Sharper than any double-edged sword, it penetrates even to dividing soul and spirit, joints and marrow; it judges the thoughts and attitudes of the heart.*
NLT	*For the word of God is alive and powerful. It is sharper than the sharpest two-edged sword, cutting between soul and spirit, between joint and marrow. It exposes our innermost thoughts and desires.*

The reading of Scripture yields a two-fold advantage for you as the reader. First, it makes you wiser by informing your mind. Second, it leads you away from the vanities and distractions of this world and points you toward the love of God. (Barclay [1972] 1997)

> The Word of God is not simply a vehicle for communicating ideas, it is living, life changing, and dynamic as it works in us. With the incisiveness of a surgeon's knife, God's word reveals who we are and what we are not.
> —*NIV Bible 2011, p. 2706*

The Bible enables you to change your way of seeing God, others, and yourself through the renewing of your mind (see Scripture #6). When you discover the power and truth of God's Word, you will begin to see changes in your life that only this truth can bring. You will even learn how to recognize what the enemy tries to bring against you. (Meyer 2015; Radiant Church 2015)

Scripture 6: **Romans 12:2 and James 1:21**

ESV	**Romans 12:2** *Do not be conformed to this world, but be transformed by the renewal of your mind, that by testing you may discern what is the will of God, what is good and acceptable and perfect.* **James 1:21** *Therefore put away all filthiness and rampant wickedness and receive with meekness the implanted word, which is able to save your souls.*

CSB	*Romans 12:2 Do not be conformed to this age, but be transformed by the renewing of your mind, so that you may discern what is the good, pleasing, and perfect will of God. James 1:21 Therefore, ridding yourselves of all moral filth and evil, humbly receive the implanted word, which is able to save you.*
NIV	*Romans 12:2 Do not conform to the pattern of this world, but be transformed by the renewing of your mind. Then you will be able to test and approve what God's will is— his good, pleasing and perfect will. James 1:21 Therefore, get rid of all moral filth and the evil that is so prevalent and humbly accept the word planted in you, which can save you.*
NLT	*Romans 12:2 Don't copy the behavior and customs of this world, but let God transform you into a new person by changing the way you think. Then you will learn to know God's will for you, which is good and pleasing and perfect. James 1:21 So, get rid of all the filth and evil in your lives, and humbly accept the word God has planted in your hearts, for it has the power to save your souls.*

The Bible is chock full of good and practical instructions on how to live your life. Not only will taking such advice to heart make you more virtuous, but you'll very likely be happier and healthier.

Those who would increase in the knowledge of God must both humble themselves before the Spirit of truth as well as commit themselves to a lifetime of study. But don't freak out. Once you start, it becomes addictive, and you can't wait to do it each day. (Bell & Campbell 2003; Stott 1999)

To Sustain Your Life
The Bible provides revelation, meditation, and nutrition for you. For you to sustain hopes and moral ideals, you must have constant, accessible, and authoritative instruction from God. This, in a nutshell, is what the Bible does. (ESV Study Bible 2011; Radiant Church 2015)

To Know Yourself
The Bible helps you see yourself more clearly. More to the point, it helps you see yourself as God sees you. While the Bible can point out the darker side of your humanity, part of its greatness is that it also shows you your potential for godliness. It teaches you that you have value. (Bell & Campbell 2003)

To Increase Your Leadership
Knowledge of the Bible can make you a more literate person, as well as a more authoritative one. The ability to cite specific quotes or give an applicable example from Scripture goes a long way to support your opinion. An awareness of what's in the Bible helps you speak with authority. (Bell & Campbell 2003)

Be careful, however, that you are not cherry-picking your Scriptures. Cherry-picking involves finding the translation and the exact words from a verse that support the point of view you are promoting. It has been said many times by many people, you can usually use almost any verse to support almost any point of view. However, if the people you are trying to convince do a little research, and you have cherry-picked your verse without regard for its context, ultimately you will decrease your authority in the eyes of others. This will have a decidedly negative effect on how people view you as a leader. (Bell & Campbell 2003)

It is Culturally Enduring
From its earliest days, the church gave priority to the reading of the Holy Scriptures. The Bible has been a cultural influence for hundreds of years. It has been and still is reflected in the art, literature, and music of the entire world. (ESV Study Bible 2011; Fee & Stuart 2014)

The Bible is at once a human book—because it was written by mortal men—and a divine book— because it was inspired by God—with eternal relevance: God is the same yesterday, today, and tomorrow (see Scripture #7). You can ignore the Bible's teachings if you want, but its stories, parables, and poetry will always be part of our cultural heritage. You lose out if you ignore such a treasure trove. (Bell & Campbell 2003; Fee & Stuart 2014; Stott 1999)

***Scripture 7:* Hebrews 13:8**

ESV; NIV; CSB; NLT	*Jesus Christ is the same yesterday and today and forever.*

How you seek to receive the message of the Bible is not the most crucial factor. But it is vital that, in some way, at some time, on a regular basis, you learn to acquire and listen to God's Word and to feed upon it in your heart. (Stott 1999)

Mini Lesson

Chapter six addresses how to study the Bible in more detail, but if you don't want to wait to give it a shot, here is a *very* brief overview.

The four key logistical factors are: period, place, prayer and process.

PERIOD: Determine a time period in which to read or study. The time period not only consists of how long and how often, but also what time of day. It is a good idea to be systematic in your reading or studying.

PLACE: Determine a specific place to study. The place should be comfortable, but as free from distractions and electronics (except a computer if you work that way) as possible. It also should be somewhere that you can keep your study tools, which are discussed in chapter four.

PRAYER: Always start and end with prayer. To begin, pray that God will grant you wisdom and that the Holy Spirit will open your spiritual eyes and ears so that you are receptive to what He is trying to tell you. You also may need to confess and repent if there are issues that might be blocking the flow of the Spirit. One of the best ways to determine if there is blockage is to ask God if anything is standing in the way of hearing Him clearly.

When you are done with your session, close with prayer. Thank God for any revelations He gave you and ask Him if there is anything else He wants you to know. Write down what you hear Him say.

PROCESS: Process refers to what you read or study. You can choose a particular book of the Bible (John is a good one to start with), or you can choose a prepared devotional or Bible reading plan. There are several to choose from on YouVersion, which is both a web site (www.bible.com) and an application that can be downloaded from the web site.

Summary

In this chapter, you learned why it is important to read or study the Bible. In short, it is the only true way to come to know the triune God—the Father, the Son and the Holy Spirit. It is your path to salvation and eternal life. Additionally, it has the capacity to change your life while on earth.

Coming Attractions

In chapter two you will learn about the Bible's demographics. The logistics, characteristics, and organization of the Bible will be discussed.

Points to Ponder

1. Of all the reasons given to read or study the Bible, list the two reasons that spoke to you the most. Explain why.

2. Graphé, Logos and Rhema are all the Word of God. In your own words, describe the differences between them.

3. In your own words, explain the difference between inspiration, revelation, and authority as they relate to the Bible.

4. Compose a closing prayer asking God what He wants you to take away from this chapter. Then be still and listen. Write down whatever you think He is saying to you.

2

What is This Thing Called Bible?

Overview of the Bible

This chapter provides information that is foundational in understanding the Bible. When you read or study the Bible, it is important to have an idea of the big picture as well as of how it is put together. This will help you make more sense of it as you tackle the various parts of the book. So, this chapter focuses on the nuts and bolts of the Bible, or, if you will, the *demographics* of the Bible: how and when it was put together; how it is organized; what the apocrypha is; other miscellaneous tidbits that are important to know.

Prayer

Father God, thank you for your love and for the desire you have put in my heart to know you better. Help me maintain my enthusiasm as I learn about the nuts and bolts of your Word. I realize that the more I know about the structure of the Bible, the better I will understand it. Holy Spirit, open my spiritual eyes and ears to see what You have to teach me today. I ask this in the name of Jesus. Amen.

Chapter Verse: *Romans 15:4*

CSB	*For whatever was written in the past was written for our instruction, so that we may have hope through endurance and through the encouragement from the Scriptures.*
NIV	*For everything that was written in the past was written to teach us, so that through the endurance taught in the Scriptures and the encouragement they provide we might have hope.*
NLT	*Such things were written in the Scriptures long ago to teach us. And the Scriptures give us hope and encouragement as we wait patiently for God's promises to be fulfilled.*

Coming to Terms with Terms

APOCALYPSE: Something viewed as a prophetic revelation, often using symbolic or figurative language.

APOCRYPHA: Secret, not part of the canon. Things which ought to be kept hidden away.

CANON RULE OR STANDARD: An authoritative list of books accepted as Holy Scripture.

COVENANT, COVENANTAL: An association between two parties with various responsibilities, benefits, and penalties. A formal, solemn, and binding agreement.

GENRE: A category of artistic, musical, or literary composition characterized by a particular style, form or content.

PROPHECY, PROPHETIC: *Verb*: To speak God's message to the people, under the influence of the Holy Spirit.

    Noun: An inspired message, sometimes encouraging obedience to God, sometimes proclaiming the future as a warning to preparedness and continued obedience. Again, offered under the influence of the Holy Spirit.

Logistics of the Bible

The Bible may appear, to the naked eye, to be a single book, but, in actuality, an entire library lies between its covers. Technically speaking, the Bible:

- is a collection of 66 books;
- was written in three languages (Hebrew, Greek, Aramaic);
- was written over a period of about 1,600 years (not consecutive);
- was produced by 40 authors writing to remarkably diverse audiences;
- was written on three different continents; and
- uses numerous *GENRES*.

While the writing of the Bible took around 1,600 years, the actual span of history covered was approximately 3,000 years. How would you like to be the project manager of that venture? Well, God did it perfectly. (Bell & Campbell 2003; ESV Study Bible 2011; Radiant Church 2015)

Those 66 books are divided into two separate collections, the Old Testament (OT) and the New Testament (NT). Actually, between the ending of Malachi—last book of the OT—and the beginning of Matthew—first book of the NT—is a span of about 400 years. You'll get more info on that later. (Bell & Campbell 2003; ESV Study Bible 2011)

Each collection (OT and NT) will be covered separately. For each collection, you will learn about the number of books it contains, the timing of those books, any other pertinent history of the collection as well as the genres of the collection—not necessarily in that order.

Old Testament

The Old Testament consists of 39 books. There are three primary genres in the OT: the law (5 books), the writings (17 books), and the prophets (17 books). All of the books are arranged according to these three genres. Within those genres, broadly speaking, are three primary subgenres: history, poetry, and *PROPHECY*. The subgenres cross over the genres. See Table 1 for a breakdown of the OT books by genre and sub-genre(s). (Barclay [1972] 1997; Bell & Campbell 2003; Stott 1999)

TABLE 1: CATEGORIES AND GENRES IN THE OLD TESTAMENT

Book	Genre	Sub-Genre	Book	Genre	Sub-Genre
Genesis	Law	History	Ecclesiastes	Writings	Poetic/Wisdom
Exodus	Law	History	Solomon	Writings	Poetic/Wisdom
Leviticus	Law	History	Isaiah	Prophecy	Major Prophet
Numbers	Law	History	Jeremiah	Prophecy	Major Prophet
Deuteronomy	Law	History	Lamentations	Prophecy	Major Prophet
Joshua	Writings	History/Prophecy	Ezekiel	Prophecy	Major Prophet
Judges	Writings	History/Prophecy	Daniel	Prophecy	Major Prophet
Ruth	Writings	History	Hosea	Prophecy	Minor Prophet
1 Samuel	Writings	History/Prophecy	Joel	Prophecy	Minor Prophet
2 Samuel	Writings	History/Prophecy	Amos	Prophecy	Minor Prophet
1 Kings	Writings	History/Prophecy	Obadiah	Prophecy	Minor Prophet
2 Kings	Writings	History/Prophecy	Jonah	Prophecy	Minor Prophet
1 Chronicles	Writings	History	Micah	Prophecy	Minor Prophet
2 Chronicles	Writings	History	Nahum	Prophecy	Minor Prophet
Ezra	Writings	History	Habakkuk	Prophecy	Minor Prophet
Nehemiah	Writings	History	Zephaniah	Prophecy	Minor Prophet
Esther	Writings	History	Haggai	Prophecy	Minor Prophet
Job	Writings	Poetic/Wisdom	Zechariah	Prophecy	Minor Prophet
Psalms	Writings	Poetic/Wisdom	Malachi	Prophecy	Minor Prophet
Proverbs	Writings	Poetic/Wisdom			

As noted in Table 1, the first five books of the Bible are considered the law. They also are known as the Pentateuch—which simply means five scrolls—and make up the Jewish Torah.

Originally, the Bible was written on scrolls, with each scroll consisting of one book. The exceptions were the longer books: Samuel, Kings, and Chronicles. These books were originally unified and taught as three books, but each was too long to be written on a single scroll, so the scribes had to write each book on two scrolls. Therefore, we now have six books. (Bell & Campbell 2003)

The current Old Testament is composed of books which, before they entered the realm of Scripture, had stood the test of many years as sacred writings. The process that established the books of the OT as Scripture started in about 621 BC. It ended with the Council of Jamnia in 90 AD. (Barclay [1972] 1997)

New Testament

When talking with people, they usually express a preference for reading the New Testament rather than the Old Testament. Not only is the news much better (salvation versus law), but it is also more accessible and understandable than the OT. New believers are encouraged to start with the NT for these very reasons. Important as it is, the OT, due to the lists and the laws it contains, can be a daunting task to the most spiritual of Christians. (Grace to You 2015)

The NT was all written within a single generation several centuries after the OT was completed. The earliest book of the NT was Galatians written in 49 AD. While there is debate about the exact timing, the latest book was 2 Peter written somewhere between 60 AD and 120 AD. (Barclay [1972] 1997; ESV Study Bible 2011)

A key fact to remember is that Christianity was born into a non-literary civilization—having no written language. There were few written documents, and it was well before the invention of the printing press. In the East, where Christianity originated, it was much more natural to transmit knowledge and teaching by word of mouth than on the printed page. At the time, the Apostles and their immediate associates were the living books on which the Gospel message was written, and through whom it was spread throughout the world. You see, it was not the New Testament that produced the church, it was the church that produced the New Testament. (Barclay [1972] 1997)

The NT has 27 books with four primary genres: Gospel (4 books), history (1 book), epistle (21 books), and *APOCALYPSE* (1 book). Table 2 lists all the books, their genre and their author(s).

TABLE 2: GENRES AND AUTHORS OF NT BOOKS

Book	Genre	Author	Book	Genre	Author
Matthew	Gospel	Matthew	**1 Timothy**	Epistle	Paul
Mark	Gospel	Mark	**2 Timothy**	Epistle	Paul
Luke	Gospel	Luke	**Titus**	Epistle	Paul
John	Gospel	John	**1&2 Thessalonians**	Epistles	Paul
Acts	History	Luke	**Philemon**	Epistle	Paul & Timothy
Romans	Epistle	Paul	**Hebrews**	Epistle	Unknown
1&2 Corinthians	Epistles	Paul	**James**	Epistle	James
Galatians	Epistle	Paul	**1&2 Peter**	Epistles	Peter
Ephesians	Epistle	Paul	**1-3 John**	Epistles	John
Philippians	Epistle	Paul	**Jude**	Epistle	Jude
Colossians	Epistle	Paul & Timothy	**Revelation**	Apocalypse	John

GOSPELS: Each one of the Gospels covers the ministry of Jesus while on earth. Written by four different authors, each Gospel has a different focus for reporting the events. While they do contain historical events, none of the Gospels should be considered history in the traditional sense of the word. None of them give an exhaustive account of the life of Jesus and His works, and most of them are not in chronological order (more on this later). Luke is considered to be the Gospel that comes closest to a historical recounting of the events surrounding Jesus, but it is not complete either.

Most study Bibles have a section known as the *Harmony of the Gospels*. This is a document, usually a table, that coordinates the events of Jesus' life across all the Gospels. When you review it, you will see that, in most of the Gospels, the chronology of events does not coincide with the order of the chapter and verse numbers. An interesting project that you might undertake sometime is to read the Gospels and map out the harmonies for yourself. A template, called *Mapping the Gospels*, and instructions for doing this over a period of 21 days is included on the Google drive.

EPISTLES: The Epistles are letters written to explain the significance of Jesus' work on the cross and His resurrection, so that believers are empowered to grasp the height, depth, breadth, and width of the love of God. You will notice that most of them are written either to churches or to a specific person. Additionally, each of them was written to address a specific topic. Woven together, the themes of the Epistles teach that salvation comes from the Lord, and that Jesus, as the Christ, has redeemed his people from the guilt and bondage of sin. (Bell & Campbell 2003; ESV Study Bible 2011)

That leaves *Acts of the Apostles* and *Revelation*.

ACTS is the story of how Jesus built up His early church through His apostles and their assistants. It is the most historical book of the New Testament. I know people who will read the book of Acts multiple times per year. They do it in order to keep fresh in their minds how to do church the way that Jesus instructed the apostles to do church.

REVELATION is considered an apocalypse because it consists of visions that were given to John to tell us what will happen in the end times. He reported them, that is wrote them down, so that you would know what to expect (see Scripture #1). The issue is, all of the visions are full of all kinds of symbolism, which leads to many different interpretations by many different people. And, contrary to what many want you to think, nowhere in the Bible does it ever state specifically when these events will take place.

Scripture 1: **Revelation 1:1-2**

ESV	¹*The revelation of Jesus Christ, which God gave Him to show to His servants the things that must soon take place. He made it known by sending His angel to His servant John, ²who bore witness to the word of God and to the testimony of Jesus Christ, even to all that He saw.*
NIV	¹*The revelation from Jesus Christ, which God gave Him to show His servants what must soon take place. He made it known by sending His angel to His servant John, ²who testifies to everything he saw—that is, the word of God and the testimony of Jesus Christ.*
NLT	¹*This is a revelation from Jesus Christ, which God gave Him to show His servants the events that must soon take place. He sent an angel to present this revelation to His servant John, ²who faithfully reported everything He saw. This is His report of the word of God and the testimony of Jesus Christ.*

OTHER GENRES? You should be aware that, in addition to the primary genres and subgenres listed above, much of the literature on the Bible will list other genres. In my opinion, many of them are more description than genre. Other terms used are narrative, homily/liturgy, biography, practical philosophy, lists, genealogies, and visions. (Barclay [1972] 1997; Bell & Campbell 2003; Stott 1999)

According to the Merriam-Webster (2014) definition, the only *genres* in that list would be homily/liturgy and biography. Any of the others are merely describing the method of delivery, and could, conceivably exist in any of the genres.

The In-Between

You come to the end of Malachi and you are proud of yourself that you finished the OT. That is a huge accomplishment! You decide a celebration is in order and head for your favorite food. The next day you return to read the next book of the Bible. You find the end of Malachi and you turn the page that says *New Testament* to find Matthew.

In the act of turning the page, you have just traversed about 400 years. God was, effectively, silent for 400 years. During that time, major political periods came and went. The culture changed drastically as the political authority changed hands from the Persians to the Greeks, to the Jewish Hasmoneans, and finally to the Romans. So, the time of Matthew was a far cry from the time of Malachi. Most study Bibles will have more in-depth information on this. Additionally, there are many books to be found covering the period between the testaments. Too numerous to mention here, you can search any library site using the subject APOCRYPHA to find some titles.

The Who-o-o-o-ole Thing

For most of the books of the Bible, they were known, used, and loved long before they were designated as sacred Scripture. Originally, the books were straightforward accounts, moving from beginning to end as any other book might. However, it was decided that referencing specific sections should be made easier, so the chapter breaks and verses within the chapters were added. This led to the Bible format that is prevalent today in both the Protestant and Catholic world. (Barclay [1972] 1997; Bell & Campbell 2003)

The Bible as we know it, containing the 66 books, was finalized in the middle of the fourth century (367 AD). That is when the CANON of Holy Scripture was closed as to which books were in and which books were out of the Bible. Since that time, no book has been added and no book has been taken away. (Barclay [1972] 1997; Bell & Campbell 2003)

Even though there have been discoveries of other documents, the content of the Bible has not changed over the years. The new discoveries serve to validate what is already there. The Dead Sea Scrolls that were discovered in the 1940s predated most existing OT copies by about 1,000 years. When existing Hebrew manuscripts were compared to these earlier documents, the faithfulness of the text was confirmed. Additionally, the reliability of the NT writings is less questionable than most secular works of the same era. (Bell & Campbell 2003)

The Apocrypha

There are ancient writings that occupy a curiously elusive position as they are neither wholly Scripture nor wholly non-Scripture. By definition *apocrypha* refers to things that ought to be kept secret or hidden away. The 2014 edition of the Merriam-Webster dictionary maintains this definition. However, in its common usage today, the word is used to denote that something is fictitious. (Merriam-Webster 2014)

The Apocrypha contains 15 books, although there are some references that count either 13 or 12 by combining some of the books. Most of those books are included in the canon of the Orthodox and Roman Catholic traditions, and excerpts from them are still read regularly in some Anglican churches. Within some Bible translations, they appear in a separate section between OT and NT; in other translations they are placed as part of some of the OT books. Most mainstream Bibles, however, do not contain any part of the Apocrypha. (Barclay [1972] 1997; ESV Study Bible 2011)

The Apocrypha, along with other writings of the times, can be helpful in limited ways. They provide the earliest interpretations of the OT literature, they explain what happened in the time between the two Testaments, and they introduce customs, ideas, and expressions that provide a helpful background when reading the NT. (ESV Study Bible 2011)

Though much in the Apocrypha simply reflects Judaism as it was practiced during a time somewhat later than the OT, there also are certain misleading passages that have historical interest. However, in terms of Christian theology and practice, they should be avoided. Therefore, the Apocrypha must be read with discretion and taken with a grain of salt. (ESV Study Bible 2011)

Characteristics of the Bible

CANONICAL: Canon, by definition, is a rule or a standard. The Canon of Scriptures is a list of books which have been accepted as the Christian Church's written rule of faith. It is the list of the official books of the Church, which it regards as authoritative and determinative for the story of its own history as well as for the formation of its life and doctrine. That is a very roundabout way of saying that the canon of the Bible contains everything God wanted you to know about Him and about how to live this life. The Canon consists of books which have the active power of guiding and directing the life and the work of the Church. And you are the Church. (Barclay [1972] 1997; ESV Study Bible 2011)

The message of God's Canon is that people should learn to love, to worship, and to serve Him. Additionally, He wants his people to live in love and to care for, as well as serve, one another as it was exemplified by Jesus. (ESV Study Bible 2011)

INSPIRATIONAL: As inspirational documents, the Bible has a divinely effected uniqueness that is comparable to the uniqueness of the incarnate Lord. All of Scripture is a witness to God, and points to Jesus. It was given to human writers who were divinely illuminated to set down on paper what God directed them to. It is God witnessing about Himself in and through their words. (Barclay [1972] 1997; ESV Study Bible 2011)

To truly understand inspiration, you must look to the divine-human situation. It is within the connection established between the Spirit of God and the mind (or spirit) of man where you will find the meaning of inspiration. This connection is established initially when you accept Jesus as your Lord and Savior. However, you need to maintain this connection through reading and studying Scripture and allowing the Holy Spirit to reveal to you the will of God through His Holy Words. (Barclay [1972] 1997)

UNIFIED: There is a great diversity of content, style, and purpose among the various books of the Bible. However, there also is demonstrable unity of their contents. In setting down His Words, God chose and inspired people, gathered from all walks of life, from many different eras, who employed various literary styles such as poetry, prophecy, history. Even with 40 different authors, 1600 years in the writing, in three different languages, the Bible does not contradict itself. Further, it reiterates the same message throughout all the books. (ESV Study Bible 2011; Stott 1999)

COVENANTAL/EDUCATIVE: In general, the process God uses to speak to us is both *COVENANTAL* and educative. It is covenantal in that He tells you that you are chosen; you are a part of His people. He promises you—makes a covenant with you—that if you are loyal to Him, you will have a greater future than you can imagine.

It is educative as God works to change you into the holy selfhood that He created you to be, the selfhood that expresses God's moral likeness. In other words, He is teaching you to be the person He created you to be. (ESV Study Bible 2011; Grace to You 2015)

Organization of the Bible

Earlier in the chapter, you learned that the OT is organized according to the categories of the books. Likewise, the different genres of the NT are grouped together. Yet, even within the same genre (i.e., the Gospels), the stories of the Bible are not chronological.

If you want to read the stories in the order that they happened, there are a couple of options. First, you could purchase a chronological Bible. This is a Bible that is organized not by the traditional method, but by the order in which the events occurred. While it makes reading the Bible more like reading a novel, the drawback is that it is very difficult to look up a specific Scripture reference. Plus, there is the cost associated with the purchase of another Bible.

A second option, and one I would recommend, is to use a reading plan that lists the scriptures in the order that, when you read them as listed, the events are in chronological order. You can then use the plan to read the stories in the order they occurred. This plan is available, with instructions on how to use it, on the Google drive. See the *URLs for Websites and Supplemental Resources* in Appendix A for the URL.

Summary

In this chapter, you learned about the logistics, characteristics, and organization of the Bible. You learned that

- there are 66 books divided into the Old Testament (39 books) and the New Testament (27 books),
- the writing of the Bible took about 1,600 years actual writing time, but spanned a time frame of many thousands of years,
- it was written by multiple authors
- it was written in three different languages,
- with all that, the Bible is completely unified, and
- it never contradicts itself.

Coming Attractions

In chapter three, you will be given information that will help you select the Bible that is perfect for you. You will learn about the different translations as well as other features that are offered that you will need to consider as part of your purchase.

Use this area for notes.

Points to Ponder

1. Write down the top two pieces of information from this chapter that were significant to you or surprised you the most. Explain why.

2. In your own words, write a brief review of how the bible is organized.

3. Briefly discuss the thoughts you had when you read about the Apocrypha.

4. Compose a closing prayer asking God what He wants you to take away from this chapter. Then be still and listen. Write down whatever you think He is saying to you.

3

Decisions, Decisions, Decisions

Choices in Bibles

Within this chapter you will find the information you need to make an informed choice when it comes to purchasing a Bible. People vary widely in the use of their Bible(s). On one end of the spectrum are those who have only one Bible and they use it for everything. It is well worn and well-marked up with lots of notations in the margins. I knew a person who was so attached to her Bible that included her notes and highlights, that she paid more than a new Bible would cost to have it repaired when it got to the point that the pages and the cover were loose. On the other end are those who purchase a Bible in every possible translation and make notes in all of them. How you use your Bible(s) is a very personal thing. There is no wrong way as long as you are extracting God's truth from the pages.

In discussing which Bible might be best for you, I will address the different translations. Additionally, you will be shown that there are several styles of Bibles along with different price ranges.

As the discussion ensues, I will use common abbreviations for the various translations. A chart linking the name of the translation to its abbreviation is found in the introductory chapter *How Does This Work?* It would be beneficial to learn these abbreviations as they are standard throughout most of the literature as well as the web.

Prayer

Thank you, Father God, for your eternal love and never-ending support for me, your child, as I endeavor to know you better. Holy Spirit, open my spiritual eyes and ears so I can absorb what you have for me in this chapter. Lord Jesus, grant me your wisdom and guide me to the right decision when it comes to choosing my Bible. I ask all this in Jesus' name. Amen.

Chapter Verse: *2 Chronicles 34:30*

CSB	*The king went up to the LORD's temple with all the men of Judah and the inhabitants of Jerusalem, as well as the priests and the Levites—all the people from great to small. He read in their hearing all the words of the book of the covenant that had been found in the LORD's temple.*
NLT	*And the king went up to the Temple of the LORD with all the people of Judah and Jerusalem, along with the priests and the Levites—all the people from the greatest to the least. There the king read to them the entire Book of the Covenant that had been found in the LORD's Temple.*

Coming to Terms with Terms

FORMAL EQUIVALENCE:	Also known as word-for-word, this approach attempts to keep as close to the words and grammar of the original language as can be conveniently put into the native tongue or language (such as English) understandably.
FUNCTIONAL OR DYNAMIC EQUIVALENCE:	Also known as phrase-for-phrase, this approach is not as concerned with the grammatical form of the original language. It attempts to keep the meaning of the original language but translates it into what would be the current way of saying the same thing in contemporary English.

OPTIMAL EQUIVALENCY:	This approach uses word-for-word translation as much as possible, but if not clear it will use phrase-for-phrase. This results in a hybrid Bible.
PARAPHRASE:	This, technically, is not a translation. Here, the author starts from a text that is not the original language and puts it into his/her own words.

How's That Again? (All About Translation Philosophies)

Choosing which translation(s) you want to use is probably the most important decision you will make when purchasing a Bible. In your search for the meaning of any passage of Scripture, I advise you to use a modern translation—unless you speak the original language (Hebrew, Greek, or Aramaic). So, choose a Bible that speaks the language of the 21st century, not the 17th century (i.e., the original KJV). (Barclay [1972] 1997)

One thing to remember as you learn about the different translation philosophies is that they are not distinct definitions. All the different translations actually lay along a continuum moving from formal at one end to paraphrase at the other. There is a translation guide included on the Google drive that shows where the various translations fall on this continuum. Notice that many of the available translations fall in between the three philosophies listed here.

Formal Equivalence

FORMAL EQUIVALENCE is the philosophy where the Scriptures are translated as close to the form of the words and grammar of the original language as possible. Thus, it is often called word-for-word. This is a misnomer, however, because there are certain words or phrases where either they do not translate into understandable, conversational English or the sentence structure becomes very awkward. For example, strict adherence to the philosophy of word-for-word would translate the French phrase, "Maison blanche" into "house white." (Fee & Stuart 2014)

One advantage of this translation philosophy is that it allows you to interpret for yourself what the passage means. However, you may or may not have the background information or the tools to interpret the meaning accurately. Examples that come closest to the ideal of formal equivalence are KJV, ASV, and NASB. (Biblica.com 2014; Fee & Stuart 2014)

Functional or Dynamic Equivalence

This translation philosophy is sometimes called functional and sometimes called dynamic. For the sake of simplicity, I will call it functional.

FUNCTIONAL EQUIVALENCE, often called phrase-for-phrase or idea-for-idea, tries to remain true to the Spirit of the Scriptures. It attempts to put the words and idioms of the original language into what would be the current way of saying the same thing in today's English, all while keeping the meaning of the original language. Functional equivalence is not as concerned with the grammatical form of the original language as it is with the meaning of the original text.

These translations are usually clearer than the formal equivalencies and quite understandable. However, if the translators missed the point for the original text, they may communicate an idea foreign to the biblical text. Examples of this philosophy, in the order they fall on the translation continuum, are NIV, NLT, and GNT.

Paraphrase

A *PARAPHRASE*—also called a Free Translation—is different from an actual translation primarily in the fact that it may not start from the original language. In this case, the authors take the text of whatever translation they are using as the basis and put it into their own words. In doing so, they can bring a perspective to the text that may not have been present originally. (Fee & Stuart 2014)

Because paraphrases aren't quite as true to the original, the translators are able to update certain phrases, throw in a little slang here and there, and generally provide a looser, more familiar writing style. However, a paraphrase may update the original writer so much that it becomes more of a commentary. If you are reading to get the story, this might be okay, but if you are studying to get the meaning, you should check with a translation that is closer to functional or even formal. (Bell & Campbell 2003; Fee & Stuart 2014)

However, if you decide you do want a paraphrase, two of the most popular are The Living Bible and The Message. The Living Bible is paraphrased from the American Standard Version, while the Message is paraphrased from the Greek. Another paraphrase that many people enjoy is what was originally titled *Good News* Bible but has been revised and is now The Good News Translation. (Crosswalk.com 2015)

Which Way Do I Go? (Pros and Cons of the Translation Philosophies)
With all the translations out there, it can be confusing. Here are some things to consider.

WORD VERSUS PHRASE
Translators must make choices regarding the meaning of Scripture. These are choices that may affect your understanding of the passage. Because Hebrew and Greek have idioms and concepts that are not easily translated to English, there is an ongoing critical tension about whether it is better to give a word-for-word translation or to give a thought-for-thought translation that gives a parallel idiom in the target language.

Most translators will agree that it is necessary to remain faithful to the original. But the question becomes, is it faithfulness to form (word-for-word) or faithfulness to meaning (phrase-for-phrase)? Sometimes faithfulness to one means a lack of fidelity to the other. The text becomes easier to read the further away you get from a word-for-word translation. At the same time, you are relying more on the theological, linguistic, or cultural understanding of the translators that lay readers do not always possess. (Biblica.com 2014; Fee & Stuart 2014)

THE ENVELOPE PLEASE
If you are waiting for a definitive statement of which Bible is the best, you will be disappointed. The truth is that no single translation of the Bible stands head and shoulders above the rest. (Wellman 2015)

The ESV ranks high in popularity. Its readability is better than the NKJV and its reliability ranks close to the KJV. (Wellman 2015)

Another popular version is the NIV (2011). This version is used by more seminaries and churches, and is quoted more often by Christian websites, than other translations. The NIV is an example of a modified-literal translation that began with a word-for-word translation, and then the translators modified the results to make the sentences more closely correspond to English syntax. Because of this, some do not consider it the most reliable. (Crosswalk.com 2015; Wellman 2015)

For merely reading, or for personal application, you may want to consider a functional translation. The NLT is a good example of this, although it falls closer to the paraphrase end of the continuum than the NIV does.

ANOTHER OPTION
Another translation option is called *OPTIMAL EQUIVALENCY*, which results in a hybrid Bible. The object of this philosophy is to use formal translation as much as possible, but where word-for-word is not clear in English, they opt for a phrase-for-phrase translation. This translation also incorporates new manuscript discoveries as well as many important translational footnotes.

As of the writing of this guide, there is only one Bible that uses the Optimal translation, and that is the *Christian Standard Bible* published by Holman in 1999. It was produced using a large committee with representatives from Christians around the world. The members came from many different recognized denominations as well as from churches that might be considered nondenominational.

Since there is only one Bible that uses this philosophy, it has not been adopted as an official philosophy by Bible scholars in general. However, I have been using this Bible as part of my devotionals since I discovered it as well as using it as one of the foundational translations for this guide. I find that it does indeed fall somewhere between formal (ESV) and functional (NIV).

SYNOPSIS

FORMAL EQUIVALENCE provides insight into the structures, idioms, allusions, metaphors, and word plays of the original text. This helps with:

- identifying the formal structure of the original text,
- reproducing metaphors and idioms,
- tracing recurrent words and verbal allusions, and
- identifying ambiguities in the text.

FUNCTIONAL EQUIVALENCE reproduces the meaning of the text with greater clarity and naturalness of expression. You will find:

- a priority of meaning over form,
- a naturalness of expression,
- clarity, and
- readability.

A PARAPHRASE encourages readers to hear the text with the same vivid relevance as the original audience did. There is:

- a naturalness of expression,
- clarity,
- readability, and
- a vivid relevance.

As previously mentioned, a drawback to a paraphrase is that the contemporizing of the Bible's message may risk distorting its original meaning. (Radiant Church 2015)

MULTIPLE TRANSLATIONS

If you want authenticity, it is best to use a translation rather than a paraphrase. Translations take great care to give you a precise interpretation from the original texts. Some of the more current ones are quite readable. While it is a good practice to do most of your Bible reading from one main translation, four different references recommend having at least two separate translations, one of which would be a formal translation and the second would be a functional translation. I personally own eight different translations, and frequently use them all. The problem with limiting yourself to one translation is that you are locked into one set of translation choices. Multiple translations can open up the understandability of the Scripture. (Bell & Campbell 2003; Biblica.com 2014; Fee & Stuart 2014; Wellman 2015)

HOW DO YOU CHOOSE?

So, which is the best translation for you? There is no simple answer because it depends on many factors. Before you are given the nitty gritty of how to decide, here are five tips to consider. (Wellman 2015)

- Popular does not necessarily mean accurate.
- Modern translations can become mistranslations (see Scripture #1 and notice the differences).
- Research your Bible translation. Perhaps you could ask a pastor, a Sunday school teacher, an elder or deacon, or a trusted Christian friend.

- If possible, buy a study Bible, especially if you buy only one.
- The best translation is mostly subjective. Does it speak to you?

Scripture 1: **Matthew 28:20**

NKJV	*Teaching them to observe all things that I have commanded you; and lo, I am with you always, [even] to the end of the age. Amen.*
ESV	*Teaching them to observe all that I have commanded you. And behold, I am with you always, to the end of the age.*
NIV	*And teaching them to obey everything I have commanded you. And surely, I am with you always, to the very end of the age.*
NLT	*Teach these new disciples to obey all the commands I have given you. And be sure of this: I am with you always, even to the end of the age."*
MSG	*Jesus, undeterred, went right ahead and gave his charge: "God authorized and commanded me to commission you: Go out and train everyone you meet, far and near, in this way of life, marking them by baptism in the threefold name: Father, Son, and Holy Spirit. Then instruct them in the practice of all I have commanded you. I'll be with you as you do this, day after day after day, right up to the end of the age."*

The first thing to do in your research is to line up several translations, side-by-side, and compare the same verses. You should use at least two or three different verses. You can use, literally, any verses you want. If you're not sure, some suggestions are:

- Ezekiel 6:9 (vastly different from translation to translation, especially the second part of the verse).
- Matthew 24:35 (almost identical in all translations except MSG).
- Psalm 1:1 (falls in between; very similar but with some differences).

Note that, in reviewing the differences in these three verses, I used four different translations and a paraphrase: ESV, CSB, NIV, NLT, and MSG. These translations start at the formal end of the continuum and move increasingly toward the paraphrase. As you are comparing the verses of your choice, hopefully one of the translations will speak to your heart. (Bell & Campbell 2003)

After you have compared verses, read the preface of the Bible translation(s) that you are considering. This will inform you of the philosophy of the translators as well as whether the translation is likely to be more or less literal (formal versus functional versus paraphrase). Most people consider a translation that was done by a committee—like the NIV or CSB—to be more reliable than one done by a single person (like the MSG). (Fee & Stuart 2014)

In deciding what kind of translation you would like, consider what your primary purpose for the Bible will be. Do you plan to read the entire Bible, just look up individual verses, or study passages in depth? Once you've answered that question, consider which translation will make that purpose easiest as well as help you avoid misunderstandings.

Some people, especially long-established Christians, may tout the King James Version as the only Bible to have. But consider this: the KJV was translated in the 1600s, and the English language has changed significantly since then. Some words may have changed their meaning. For example, the word that is now translated "nice" was originally translated as "silly."

Other Considerations
Once you determine the translation you want, there are other aspects to consider when choosing your Bible.

What Style Do I Want?
There are several styles of Bibles available for purchase. Table 1 highlights some of the most common. This is by no means an exhaustive list. (Bell & Campbell 2003; Wellman 2015)

Table 1: Styles of Bibles

Style	References*	Pertinent Info
Compact	Yes and No	Small in size, usually with very small typeface. It can be purchased with or without references.
Personal	Yes and No	Larger than the compact, but still small enough to be easily carried. Typeface can be small. It can be purchased with or without references.
Parallel	For some of the translations	These Bibles contain two to four different translations side-by-side on each page so that you can read the same verse in the different translations (combinations vary widely) just by moving across the page(s). This allows you to extract the meaning out of each verse. These Bibles are usually quite thick and hard bound, making them heavy.
Journaling	Yes and No	These are personal Bibles that leave plenty of white space in which to write notes and personal thoughts. You can get them with or without references.
Study	Yes, plus many other informational items	Contains extra information about the who, what, when, where, why, and how for each book. Additionally, most of the verses have study notes about how to interpret the text. There are extra maps, illustrations, and charts included. Very large and very heavy. Some are targeted to a specific demographic i.e. students, men, or women.
Application	Yes, plus many other informational items	Contains extra information about the who, what, when, where, why, and how for each book. Here, the info for the verses focuses on how to apply the text to your life. One of the features of this style is the background info that highlights the biography and actions of different people of the Bible.
Large Print	Yes and No	Most styles of Bible already listed can be obtained in large print. Be advised, the larger the print, the larger the physical book, so compact Bibles are no longer quite so compact.

*Refers to the cross-referencing of verses and translation notes within the text. Bibles usually have both or neither. Purchasing a Bible with references usually costs a little more.

Typeface might also be a consideration. Do you want or need large print to read the text comfortably? While the typeface, per se, does not add to the cost of the Bible, the larger the typeface, the larger the Bible, the more expensive it will be.

At What Cost?

The cost of your Bible will depend on many things. The absolute least expensive will be a basic Bible, without any kind of references or study helps. These Bibles are usually quite compact and easy to transport; however, they are designed for one purpose, reading.

The Bible styles listed in Table 1 go from least expensive to most expensive as far as style of Bible goes. Another factor in the cost of your Bible will be the cover. Listed in order of expense, Bibles can be found in paperback, hard cover, imitation leather, or genuine leather. The imitation leather and genuine leather can be engraved with your name for an additional cost. In general, the fewer bells and whistles the Bible has, the less expensive it will be. If your goal is simply to read through the Bible, then you can get a copy without all the extras. (Bell & Campbell 2003)

However, if you are able to purchase only one Bible, and if you plan to do more than just read the Bible, I strongly suggest a study Bible or possibly an application Bible. While it has a larger initial investment, you will glean significantly more understanding from the different passages because of the study helps that are provided than you will from a simple reference Bible. If you cannot afford a study Bible, at the minimum you should purchase a Bible with the cross-references and translation notes.

WHERE DO I GO?

Once you have determined exactly what you want (translation, style, typeface, and cover), shop around to find the best price. In addition to the brick-and-mortar stores, there are several online sites that sell Bibles.

If you want to see the book in person before you make your purchase, the best place to go is to a Christian bookstore if there is one near you. Otherwise, you can go to most large-scale book stores. They usually carry multiple styles and translations of Bibles with different covers.

Summary

There are many things to consider when purchasing your Bible(s). The most important aspect is the translation(s) that you choose. The translation affects your understanding of the Bible more than any other consideration. While size, style, and binding are key factors, they do not mean much if you are not understanding what you are reading.

The most important thing to do in choosing your Bible is to spend some time in prayer. Even if you are a newbie to Christianity, God will lead you to the one that is right for you.

Once you determine what you really want, shop around various places including the web. I have purchased 95% of my Bibles online.

Coming Attractions

Go forth and acquire your perfect Bible (or perhaps borrow one from the library or someone else). You will need a reference Bible for the next chapter which looks at the various study aids and reference tools that are available. One of the *Points to Ponder* will require you to use a reference Bible to complete the exercise.

Points to Ponder

1. Write down the top two pieces of information from this chapter that were significant to you or surprised you the most. Explain why.

2. After reading the chapter, what style of Bible do you anticipate purchasing? Explain why.

3. In your own words, explain why the Bible translation you choose is your most crucial decision in purchasing a Bible.

4. Compose a closing prayer asking God what He wants you to take away from this chapter. Then be still and listen. Write down whatever you think He is saying to you.

4

Tools of the Trade

Reference Sources for Reading or Studying the Bible

During the next few pages, you will learn about the mechanics of studying the Bible as well as some of the tools (resources) that can help you along the way. There are many different ones out there, but keep in mind that it is the quality of the tools you use—not the quantity of them—that makes your journey most productive. (ESV Study Bible 2011)

The more tools you try to use, the more time you will need for your Bible reading or study sessions. However, the more tools you use, the deeper will be your understanding of what you are reading or studying. You must find the happy medium that works for you. The key factor is to let the Holy Spirit guide you in the choice and use of what tools and resources work best for you and your studying/reading goals. (Bell & Campbell 2003; Virkler 2013)

Prayer

Father God, giver of all knowledge and wisdom, thank You for Your eternal love. Thank You, also, for Your desire to have a relationship with me and to share with me who You are. Make the concepts presented in this chapter clear to me so that I can better use these tools to read and study Your Word. I want to know You better. I ask this in Jesus' name, amen.

Chapter Verse: *Proverbs 2:5, 9*

CSB	*⁵Then you will understand the fear of the Lord and discover the knowledge of God. ... ⁹Then you will understand righteousness, justice, and integrity—every good path.*
NLT	*⁵Then you will understand what it means to fear the LORD, and you will gain knowledge of God. ... ⁹Then you will understand what is right, just, and fair, and you will find the right way to go.*

Coming to Terms with Terms

CONCORDANCE: A list of key words, along with some of the verses where the word appears, that will help you narrow your search for verses.

EXHAUSTIVE CONCORDANCE: A list of every word in the Bible along with all the verses where each word appears.

GOODRICK/ KOHLENBERGER: The word numbering system used in The NIV Exhaustive Bible Concordance. (2015)

In-Bible Tools

Almost every Bible comes with some tools embedded into them. These include, at a minimum, cross-references for verses, footnotes with translation messages or other pertinent information, and maps. Some Bibles also include a mini *CONCORDANCE* in the back. Note: It is possible to purchase a Bible that has no tools included, but for the small difference in price, I would not recommend it. **Read the pages in the front of the Bible** to discover which tools it contains and how they are used.

Biblical Notations

There are a multitude of abbreviations used by Bibles in order to preserve space. All the abbreviations used within your Bible are presented on a page in the beginning of the publication. Mark that page as you will refer to it frequently. Note that some of the abbreviations and notations will vary from Bible to Bible, but others are pretty standard across platforms. Some of the more common ones are listed below.

- **cf.:**   Compare. Usually leads you to another verse that means the same thing or uses the same translation for a word.
- **ch, chs.:**   Chapter or chapters.
- **f., ff.:**   Following verse or following verses.
- **Lit.:**   Literally
- **v., vv.:**   Verse or verses.

Other notations include how cross-references are indicated and how footnotes are indicated. Some Bibles also make notations in either the Old Testament, the New Testament, or both, on verses that refer to prophecies that were given in the OT and then fulfilled in the NT. However, each Bible uses its own system of notations, so **be sure to read the front of your Bible** to learn the system particular to your edition.

Using Cross-References

The cross-reference system in a Bible is designed, primarily, to lead you to similar verses elsewhere in the text. These are handy because you can start with one verse and build a whole study by following all the cross-references from verse to verse (sometimes called the spider web technique). Sometimes this can be a short endeavor because the two verses only reference each other, but it can be a quite enlightening adventure if the trail is long enough.

Generally, there are four types of cross-references: (ESV Study Bible 2011)

- references to specific words or phrases that appear in other verses,
- comparative references that direct the reader to passages with the same theme,
- less direct references that provide additional information or insight to the verse, and
- quoted references that indicate the source for verses or phrases quoted from other places in the Bible. For example, there are many places in the NT where the authors use quotes from the OT. Jesus did this a lot.

Again, your Bible may include some or all these cross-reference types. You must **read the beginning pages** to find out which ones you have and how they are notated.

There is one thing to be aware of when using your cross-reference system, and that is the closer your translation is to formal equivalence, the more in-depth the system will be, especially when using key words and concepts.

Using Footnotes

Footnotes are included in the Bible to give various explanations. There are generally four types of footnotes provided. (ESV Study Bible 2011)

ALTERNATIVE TRANSLATIONS are provided for specific words or phrases when there is a strong possibility that such words or phrases could be translated in another way. Since translation from the original language into English is not exact due to the differences in the languages, the translation most likely to preserve the meaning is used within the text; then a footnote is provided to inform you of a possible alternate translation.

EXPLANATIONS OF GREEK AND HEBREW TERMS relate primarily to the meaning of specific Greek or Hebrew terms. These include the meaning of names, a literal translation that is too awkward to be used in the English text, as well as notes that indicate either that an absolute certainty of the meaning of a word or phrase is not possible, or that there is a specialized use of a Greek word.

MISCELLANEOUS EXPLANATORY NOTES that may be provided can:

- clarify additional meanings of words or phrases that may not be apparent otherwise;
- provide important grammatical points that would not otherwise be apparent in English, when the referent for a pronoun has been supplied in the English text; or
- provide notes giving English equivalents of weights, measurements, and monetary values.

TECHNICAL TRANSLATION NOTES indicate how translation decisions have been made when dealing with difficult Hebrew and Greek passages. These can include some very technical terms. If you want an explanation of them, you will need to find a standard Bible study reference that talks about the terms.

Again, your Bible may or may not have all these types of footnotes. **Read the front of your Bible** to find out what it does and does not include.

Using a Concordance

Many Bibles will have a mini concordance in the back. A full description of a CONCORDANCE is given below. One drawback to the in-Bible concordance is that, due to space, it cannot be exhaustive. Therefore, the editors make choices of what words will appear as well as which of the verses they will list for each word. For example, I looked up the word *faith* in four of my personal resources. The ESV reference Bible listed 31 verses. The NKJV reference Bible listed 11 verses. The CSV study Bible listed 34 verses. But the EXHAUSTIVE CONCORDANCE (based on the KJV) listed 245 verses.

The use of various concordances is pretty standard, but you still should **read the front of your Bible** in case there are special instructions.

Useful Tools and References

There are a multitude of tools and references you can use to aid you in your study of the Bible. I will cover seven of them.

Exhaustive Concordance

A concordance contains key words, listed alphabetically, followed by a list of the verses in the Bible where that word is found. An exhaustive concordance contains *every* word in the Bible along with *every* verse where that word appears. It is useful in conducting word studies where you can quickly accumulate a comprehensive understanding of key themes (forgiveness, repentance, salvation, etc.). If you want to do a topical Bible study, the concordance is your best friend. (Bell & Campbell 2003)

However, I use it mostly when I am thinking of a passage for which I cannot remember the chapter and verse reference. I look up the most prominent (and unique) key word in the verse to find where it appears.

An exhaustive concordance provides additional information that in-Bible concordances do not. It provides the words in the original language as well as the translation(s)—aka definitions—from that language. This is helpful if you are having a tough time understanding exactly what the verse means. There are two sets of translations, Greek and Hebrew. This is because most of the OT is written in Hebrew, while most of the NT is written in Greek.

The original words, along with their definitions appear at the back of the concordance. Each word is numbered, and that number appears at the end of the word listing in the main part of the concordance. If the number is *italicized*, it is in the Greek section. If it is in normal text, it appears in the Hebrew section. If you have trouble remembering which is which, remember that OT =

Hebrew (plain old text) and NT = Greek (italicized). See Table 1 for the listing from *Strong's Exhaustive Concordance* of the first six verses that appear for the word *faith*.

Not long ago, the only exhaustive concordance around was *Strong's*, which is based on the KJV. However, today there are excellent concordances for both NIV and GNB as well as a *Strong's* for NASB. I cannot speak to the contents of the GNB or NASB. The NIV, in addition to original words and their translations, provides two cross-reference tables: one starts with *Strong's* and gives the word number for the G-K (*GOODRICK/KOHLENBERGER*) system, the other starts with the G-K and provides the word number for *Strong's* system.

Note that, because they are two different translations, there is not a one-to-one relationship between *Strong's* and the G-K system as some words appear in one that do not appear in the other. See Table 2 for the listing from The *NIV Exhaustive Bible Concordance* of the first three verses that appear for the OT & NT for the word *faith*. Note: The NIV has 10 entries from the OT instead of just two, so I used just the first three to show you some from Matthew also.

Table 1: Example from Strong's Exhaustive Concordance

De	39:20	Children in whom is no *f.*	529
Hab	2: 4	But the just shall live by his *f.*	530
M't	7:30	More clothe you, O ye of little *f?*	*3640*
M't	8:10	I have not found so great *f,* no, not	*4102*
M't	8:26	Are ye fearful, O ye of little *f?*	*3640*
M't	9: 2	Jesus seeing their *f* said unto the	*4102*

Note that the word *faith* is translated four separate ways in these verses.

Table 2: Example from the NIV Exhaustive Concordance

Ex	21: 8	because he has **broken f** with her.	H953
Dt	32:51	is because both of you **broke f** with me in	H5085
Jos	22:16	how could you **break f** with the	H5085 +5086
Mt	6:30	not much more clothe you—you **of little f?**	*G3899*
Mt	8:10	found anyone in Israel with such great **f.**	*G4411*
Mt	8:26	He replied, "You of **little f**, why are you so	*G4411*

See the front of the *NIV Exhaustive Bible Concordance* (2015) for an explanation of why multiple words are bolded.

Learning to use your concordance efficiently and effectively takes practice. I don't know of anyone who conquered it right away. So, have faith (no pun intended). You will get the hang of it. Once you do, I pray that you are as excited about the study possibilities it opens up as I am.

An exhaustive concordance is expensive. Therefore, you'll probably only want to purchase one to begin with. If you chose the NIV Bible translation, you should get the NIV concordance, because there are enough differences in translation to make using the Strong's concordance frustrating. If you opted for the ESV, then the Strong's is your best bet. If you have chosen a different translation (like NLT or CSB) then take your Bible (or a list of words from the Bible) to the store and look them up in both versions to determine which one will work the best for you.

Vine's Concise Dictionary of the Bible

If you cannot afford an exhaustive concordance, but you want more information about what the words mean, check out *Vine's Concise Dictionary of the Bible* (2005). It contains key words and phrases of the Bible, but it is by no means an exhaustive list. For each word, it will tell you the part of speech it belongs to (noun, verb, adverb, etc.), as well as the original word and the *Strong's* definition reference number separated by Old and New Testament entries.

That information is followed by the definitions taken from Strong's with a few of the Scripture references where it appears using that definition. It also shows multiple entries if it has multiple definition reference numbers. For example, *faith* shows one OT entry (definition number 530), and two NT entries (one definition number 4102 and one definition number 3640).

The cost of Vine's is not exorbitant. I usually look at Vine's before going to the concordance because it is more informative and easier to read than the concordance. But, since it is not exhaustive, it is limiting in that the word you are researching may not appear.

Regular Dictionary

One of the most useful tools, and one of the most overlooked for Bible study, is a plain old dictionary—the kind you have been using since elementary school. Many strange biblical words are well interpreted in a modern dictionary. Any dictionary will work, but I recommend the *Merriam-Webster's Collegiate Dictionary*, 11th edition (2014) or a later edition.

While the editors add and remove words almost annually, it is not necessary to buy a new dictionary every year. Generally, the words that are being added and removed are colloquial or idioms and do not have much to do with Scripture.

The expense of a dictionary varies based on the features you choose. I wanted a comprehensive dictionary, with a hard cover, and large print. Therefore, my copy cost more than a paper back, pocket version.

Bible Dictionary

A Bible dictionary pertains exclusively to Bible artifacts, customs, and culture, and will give you an even better grasp about the subject. The primary one on the market is the *Holman Illustrated Bible Dictionary* (2003). Found in the Foreword, the editors stated:

> *Our sincere hope is that this book will serve multiple purposes, such as facilitating acquisition of knowledge about the Bible, understanding the Bible's meaning and message, and providing an entrée into the wider world of biblical scholarship. (Bell & Campbell 2003)*

Loaded with lots of illustrations and maps, you can dive deeply into almost any subject you can think of. However, that can make it overwhelming to the Bible study newbie who is just starting out. This, plus the expense of the volume, might suggest it is better left for later in your journey.

Bible Handbook

When you hear Bible handbook, you should think *Halley's Bible Handbook*. The completely revised and expanded 25th edition (2000) includes more illustrations and notes as well as Bible study guides and prayers.

What is the Bible handbook? First, it gives some overall background of the Bible and how it came to be. Then it takes every chapter of the Bible and provides a synopsis of the events in that chapter. Additionally, it gives background information on selected items (people, places, or events). For instance, the pages covering Matthew contain 14 information inserts covering extensive information. A few of the topics are: Mary, Joseph, Old Testament Prophecies of Christ Quoted in the Gospels, Parables, and Where Did Jesus Preach the Sermon on the Mount.

The expense is moderate; however, it is very useful in the case where you can remember a story, but you can't remember exactly in which book it appears. Since each chapter in the handbook usually consists of only a few paragraphs, it makes skimming the OT or NT to find the story much easier.

Commentaries

Commentaries, of which there are many, are the comments of a person or organization about what's in the Bible. Usually they are organized by book, chapter, and verse. One major source for these is the Blue Letter Bible website (www.blueletterbible.org). They have audio, video, and text commentaries by multiple people. The commentaries are tied to a specific verse, so if you are looking at a verse within the website, you can click on the appropriate icon and it will take you to a list of commentaries on that book, chapter, or verse. (Bell & Campbell 2003)

Another source for commentaries are the many study guides you can find on the books of the Bible or other topics (love, faith, etc.). While usually very enlightening in their teaching, they are, basically, the commentary of a person or an organization.

Beware of commentaries that appear on sites like Wikipedia. They may or may not fall in line with Scripture, which is the standard that all reputable commentaries need to meet.

Web Sites

There are several websites out there that can help you. Each one has a slightly different focus. This guide will focus on four of those sites.

YouVersion (www.bible.com)

The primary focus of YouVersion is reading the Bible. You can easily look up individual verses or whole chapters. If you are viewing a chapter, cross-reference and footnote information is provided through icons that you can hover over or click on. You can easily change the translation you are reading.

YouVersion has more translations of the Bible than any other site I have seen. Many of the versions have audio so you can listen to the Bible as you read it. The site also has the ability to view the Bible in parallel, but only with two different translations.

The site has two other features that are useful. First, it provides a Verse of the Day. Each day it posts a new verse for contemplation and prayer. You can have this verse emailed to you in the translation of your choice. Second, the site provides a multitude of devotional studies, ranging in length from three days to 30 or more days (very few go beyond 30 days). There is a wide range of topics, so there is something for everyone.

Crosswalk (www.crosswalk.com)

This website focuses on life application of the Scriptures. The following description and quote were taken directly from the web site's *About Us* page.

> *Crosswalk.com aims to offer the most compelling biblically based content to Christians on their walk with Jesus. Crosswalk.com is your online destination for all areas of Christian Living—faith, family, fun, and community. Each category is further divided into areas important to you and your Christian faith including Bible study, daily devotions, marriage, parenting, movie reviews, music, news, and more.*

> We believe that the Christian faith isn't just for Sunday mornings in Church; our faith informs every issue we face every day of the week. We want to provide content to people who are seeking to determine what living Christianity day-to-day means in their own lives.

Bible Study Tools (www.biblestudytools.com)

The primary advantage of Bible study tools is that it provides multiple plans for reading through the Bible. There are topical, chronological, straight through, and more. The plans go from 90 days to 2 years. Some cover the whole Bible, while some focus on the New Testament. The three plans contained on the Google drive for reading the Bible in a year were originally obtained from this site; however, I have modified them slightly. One reason for the modification was to make the chronology better; another reason was to even out the amount of reading per day.

Another feature of this site is that it provides descriptions of, and links to, multiple study tool devices (concordances, commentaries, lexicons, etc.).

Blue Letter Bible (www.blueletterbible.com)

If your desire is to delve as deeply into the Bible as you can, then Blue Letter Bible (BLB) is the site for you. While it does not contain as many translations as some of the other sites, it does contain 20, six of which would be used by advanced Bible scholars. Most of the translations would be considered closer to the formal equivalence end of the continuum, although it does contain NIV and NLT.

There are two selling points for this site. First, you can look up and easily copy multiple verses at a time in any of the translations. Once retrieved, two clicks will change the verse to a different translation. This is great if you want to provide the verse text in multiple translations. You can look it up, then copy and paste it. It also is useful for listing out all the cross references for a particular verse so that they can be read all in one place.

The second, and more powerful, tool is that for every verse in the Bible you are provided with a tools icon that opens up a dialogue box with six different tool tabs, which are described below.

- Interlinear This is the concordance which includes the Hebrew/Greek Lexicon. It gives you *Strong's* word number along with the original word written in the original language, then translated into English as well as an audio file to tell you how to pronounce the word.
- Bibles Clicking on this button provides the verse in every translation provided by BLB.
- Cross Refs This takes you to a page that displays correlating verses from the Bible based on key words. It is similar to a cross-reference list in your Bible.
- Commentators This tab lists audio tools, study tools, and commentaries. It provides an extensive list of different study tools (audio, visual, and text) from which you can choose. Most of them are commentaries.
- Dictionaries Clicking on this link opens a list of links to available dictionary aids for the verse. They are topical connections from other references.
- Miscellaneous This button provides a list of hymns and images that are available which correspond to the verse.

This is only a brief review of the possible ways to use this site. I encourage you to go through the tutorials that the site offers. You will learn how to get even more out of your time with God.

People Sources
In addition to all the tools already listed, don't forget the people around you. Your pastor is a reliable source of information. If you live near a college, university, or seminary, you might be able to connect with a Bible scholar there.

Another source is to find a mature Christian, either in your church or another church, and develop a relationship with him or her. If they don't know the answer to your question, they usually have the resources to find out. Or they can direct you to a source to find the answer for yourself.

Summary
There are many tools and references available to you when you decide to study the Bible. How many of them you use will depend on how deeply you want to delve into the Scriptures as well as how much time you want to spend on Bible study each day.

Based on my own experience, you probably will use the tools contained within your Bible the most. So, **be sure to read the pages in the front of your Bible** to learn what those tools are and how to use them.

Coming Attractions
The next chapter will discuss things that are handy to know before you start reading the Bible. It also will discuss decisions that need to be made based on whether you are going to just read the Bible or whether you are going to study it.

Points to Ponder

1. Of all the tools talked about in this chapter, list the top two tools you think will work best for you. Explain why.

2. Look up Romans 3:22. Now follow all the cross-referenced verses and write them all down.

3. Use the word *faith*, or choose another word you want to know about, and look it up in your concordance. Record up to five verses that are listed, then look them up and read them.

4. Compose a closing prayer asking God what He wants you to take away from this chapter. Then be still and listen. Write down whatever you think He is saying to you.

5

Where Do I Begin and How Deep Do I Go?

(1) Bible Basics and (2) Reading vs. Studying the Bible

The purpose of this chapter is two-fold. First, there are things you need to be aware of that have to do with how you approach the Bible. Second, you will explore things to consider while you are deciding whether to study the Bible or just read it. Additionally, you will be given information on the different purposes for reading the Bible.

Prayer

Holy Father, thank You for Your wisdom and teaching. As I endeavor to learn the basics of how to read and study Your Word, fill me with an excitement and an anticipation of the adventures that lie ahead. Open my spiritual eyes and ears so that I can see and hear what You want me to know. Instill in my heart the plan You want me to follow. Help to illuminate the words on the page so that, like the Israelites, I can understand and celebrate with extraordinary joy the journey I am about to undertake. I ask this in Jesus' name. Amen.

Chapter Verse: *Nehemiah 8:8, 12*

CSB	*⁸They read out of the book of the law of God, translating and giving the meaning so that the people could understand what was read. ... ¹²Then all the people began to eat and drink, send portions, and have a great celebration, because they had understood the words that were explained to them.*
NLT	*⁸They read from the Book of the Law of God and clearly explained the meaning of what was being read, helping the people understand each passage. ... ¹²So the people went away to eat and drink at a festive meal, to share gifts of food, and to celebrate with great joy because they had heard God's words and understood them.*

Coming to Terms with Terms

BLB	Blue Letter Bible (www.blueletterbible.com) A Bible study web site.
PRECEPT	A command or principle intended as a general rule of action; what God has appointed to be done.
SPIDER WEB	A term used in research where you follow one reference to another, to another, to another. It is so named because, if laid out in a graphical representation, the end result resembles a spider web.
TOPICAL STUDY	The term used to describe the study method where you look up references based on a subject (topic) such as faith or salvation. This involves following all the cross references for the topic and may involve more than one Greek or Hebrew word.
WORD STUDY	The term used to describe the study method where you focus on a particular word such as faith or salvation. This involves studying the meaning of the word in its original language and may involve more than one topic.

Where Do I Begin?

This section discusses some topics that are important to understand and consider before you ever open your Bible.

Note: For simplicity's sake, I will use the term *read*, but understand it as *read or study*.

What you get out of the time you spend reading the Bible depends heavily on how you come to the Bible. The key is to enter God's Word with humility. Pray before you read the Scripture then read with a prayerful frame of mind. After you have read it, submit to the text and pray for understanding as well as the wisdom to apply it to your life. (Barclay [1972] 1997; Radiant Church 2015; Stott 1999)

Who You Are

Who you are and where you are in life has a significant impact on what you read. Your specific circumstances will bring distinct aspects of Scripture to life. The Holy Spirit supplies the interpretation for what you read, and He is what you need Him to be—comforter, teacher or advocate—based on your current circumstances.

> A text may have a different significance or import for me each time I turn to it. . . for the Lord will speak to me where I am.
> —*Thelma Hall (Johnson 2003)*

It is important to approach the Bible with a positive yet critical attitude. Positive means that you approach it with an open mind, ready to learn. Critical, here, means that you rely on wisdom to objectively discern what the Bible is telling you. Another important attitude is questioning, mostly questioning how what you are learning can be applied to your life. These three traits will help you grasp its central message and put it into practice.

However, you probably know more about the Bible than you realize. If you are curious about how much you already know, there is a Bible IQ quiz included in Appendix B and on the Google drive at https://docs.google.com/document/d/1GYDZ0y8Ol0swWpNtVU4HSv8GwhCG6P3Fu9NsYhH08JE/copy. The answers are found in Appendix G and on the Google drive at https://docs.google.com/document/d/16YLhj76Z2rJ7f3ImtKhIgEanNvA2OpZWF6OnA01dPZs/copy.

Come with Honesty

This does not refer to your character, exactly. It refers to the attitude with which you approach the Bible. You should come to the Bible to find God's truth, not to prove a point about which you have already made up your mind. If you go to Scripture with your mind already made up, all you are likely to hear is the reassuring echoes of your own prejudice, not the truth that God wants to impart. (Barclay [1972] 1997; Stott 1999)

> When we read the Bible, we should be very sure that we are listening for God and not for the echo of our own voice.
> —*William Barclay (Barclay [1972] 1997)*

An honest approach to Scripture encompasses the whole of Scripture. It is more challenging to attempt a basic comprehension of the entire Bible, but it is better than continually emphasizing certain portions while ignoring the rest. God wrote it all for a reason. Therefore, approach the Bible objectively, read it thoroughly, and refrain from forming strong opinions until you have seen it in its entirety. (Barclay [1972] 1997; Bell & Campbell 2003)

Come Wholeheartedly

You must take the whole of yourself—mind, heart, and spirit—to the reading of the whole of Scripture. If you seek the Lord with your whole heart, presenting all your faculties for the Lord to fill and use, you will find Him (see Scripture #1). Ask the Holy Spirit to guide you and fill your heart. Then focus on the flowing thoughts and pictures He puts in your mind as well as the emotions He elicits. (Barclay [1972] 1997; Virkler 2013)

***Scripture 1:* Jeremiah 29:13**

ESV; NIV	*You will seek me and find me, when you seek me with all your heart.*
CSB; NLT	*You will seek me and find me when you search for me with all your heart.*

God commands you to love Him with everything you have (see Scripture #2). You must read the Bible in the same way. If your goal is just to get it done, you will be anxious to complete it and you will miss out on much of what God is trying to tell you. However, if your goal is to connect with God, you might—and should—pause whenever you sense God is speaking to you. (Barclay [1972] 1997; Johnson 2003)

Scripture 2: **Luke 10:27a**

CSB; NIV	*He answered, "Love the Lord your God with all your heart, with all your soul, with all your strength, and with all your mind."*

You need to develop a solid spiritual discipline. This includes anything that helps you to practice being attentive to that small voice in your spirit. Then you need to be willing to respond when you hear it. Understand that any spiritual exercises you do must be done with the goal of understanding and connecting with God. (Johnson 2003)

Come with Reverence

Bringing a spirit of reverence to reading the Bible is essential. However, this is not the norm today. (Barclay [1972] 1997)

> Our modern approach to the Word is sometimes characterized by a certain sterility because it relies more on reason than on wisdom, more on speculative study than on participative knowledge, more on thinking than on praying.
> —*Enzo Bianchi (Johnson 2003)*

When you approach Scripture with reverence, the Holy Spirit continues to bring illumination and revelation to what you read. Serious Christian reading of the Scripture uses that reverence to seek out and find the grace of God. (Johnson 2003).

> The most precious thing a man has is his heart, his self; a heart and a self that are filled with love for God and love for man—that is the only gift God wants.
> —*William Barclay (Barclay [1972] 1997)*

How Deep Do I Go?

Whether you decide to read or to study I recommend that you use other tools, such as those discussed in chapter four, in order to gain a fuller understanding of what God is saying to you. First, read the passage in multiple translations. If you have a study Bible, read any notes that pertain to the passage. There also may be other background information provided that would help illuminate the passage. Additionally, there are many commentaries available on any passage you are reading. The most extensive collection I have found is on *BLB*.

For Your Consideration

Explanations of the items to be considered in your decision to read or study the Bible are provided in Table 1. Use it to determine which items need to be considered for reading and which for studying.

TABLE 1: CONSIDERATIONS FOR READING OR STUDYING

Point to Consider	*Reading*	*Studying*
How much time?	X	X
When do you spend the time?	X	X
Over what period of time?	X	X
What order?	X	
What is your focus?		X
Alone or Together?	X	X

How Much Time? One of the first decisions is how much time you will spend on this endeavor. You can start small with 15-30 minutes per day.

When Do I Spend the Time? Once you decide how much time, you can determine the when. There is everything to be said for regular and systematic reading of the Bible. The time of day that you read is entirely personal. But it should be a time that is set aside. Put it on your calendar like any other appointment. (Barclay [1972] 1997)

Over What Period of Time? How long do you want to take to accomplish the task? If you are reading the Bible, it may be 6 months or a year, depending on how much you are reading. If you are studying a topic, the time frame probably will be shorter and will vary based on what you are studying.

What Order? In what order do I want to read the Bible? There are many options:

- You can read it straight through.
- You can read it chronologically.
- You can read a few verses from three or four separate books each time. This method lets you mix in Psalms, Proverbs, and the NT while working your way through other OT books.

If studying, what is Your Focus? What do you want to know? Do you want to do a study that focuses on a particular book of the Bible? Do you want to do a *topical study*? Do you want to do a *word study*? All are options, and you can find material on almost anything you want to study.

Alone or Together? Whether reading or studying the Bible, it can be done either alone or with others. Both scenarios have their pros and cons. Often, a mix is the best option. You may choose to do your reading alone, but opt for studying with a group of people. Or you may choose to read alone, but do it in tandem with another person(s) and come together periodically to discuss what was read. It is possible to do in-depth studying alone, but there is agreement that there is a deeper learning when you are in a group where you can discuss different points of view and/or understandings. William Barclay ([1972] 1997) states that studying within a fellowship group is much richer because: 1) No one can find truth alone; 2) No human endeavor is effective without the Spirit and the grace of God; and 3) No conclusion is valid if it is arrived at having no regard for the fellowship of the Church.

Other Considerations

While a nice Bible can be a beautiful thing to behold, you need to read it, not just admire it. You should know, though, that no matter how much you learn, you will never learn it all. No one will until we see Jesus face-to-face (see Scripture 3). You do, however, stand a better chance of learning if you do it in the fellowship of the Church (see Scripture 4). (Barclay [1972] 1997; Bell & Campbell 2003; Grace to You 2015)

Scripture 3: 1 Corinthians 13:12

ESV	*For now, we see in a mirror dimly, but then face to face. Now I know in part; then I shall know fully, even as I have been fully known.*
NLT	*Now we see things imperfectly, like puzzling reflections in a mirror, but then we will see everything with perfect clarity. All that I know now is partial and incomplete, but then I will know everything completely, just as God now knows me completely.*

Scripture 4: 2 Peter 1:20

NIV	*Above all, you must understand that no prophecy of Scripture came about by the prophet's own interpretation of things.*
NLT	*Above all, you must realize that no prophecy in Scripture ever came from the prophet's own understanding,*

While you are reading, do it with the expectation that God will speak to you. During the process, take time to listen to what He is saying. Sometimes this takes a few minutes of quiet time. After all, God works on His own time schedule. (Johnson 2003; Stott 1999)

Types of Reading

This section will concentrate on the different focuses you can have while reading. There are three primary focuses for reading the Bible: 1) theological, 2) as literature, and 3) to be with God. (ESV Study Bible 2011)

THEOLOGICAL READING

Theological reading is done by looking for God throughout the Scriptures. Read with an emphasis on who God is—His being, His character, His words and works, His purpose, His presence, His power, His promises, and His PRECEPTS. The primary purpose for theological reading is to discern God with maximum clarity through His own testimony—i.e., Scripture—as to His will, His works, and His ways. When reading, you usually focus either on a quest for God (to know God) or on a quest for Godliness (to be like God), which really are two sides of the same coin. (ESV Study Bible 2011)

READING AS LITERATURE

Any piece of writing—Bible, fiction, poetry—needs to be interpreted in terms of the kind of writing that it is. The goal of literature is to prompt you, the reader, to vicariously share or relive an experience. In general, it can be either fact or fiction. But not the Bible, which is always fact.

Anything having to do with how a biblical author has expressed his message constitutes literary form. Understanding these literary forms—genres or approaches—will make you aware of how much the Bible challenges your world today. Note: I discuss genres of the Bible in more depth in chapters seven and eight. (Barclay [1972] 1997; ESV Study Bible 2011)

The bottom line is that the literature of the Bible cannot quite be fit into the categories that have been invented to describe other literature. The implication for interpreting the Bible as literature is that readers and expositors (i.e., you) need to actively recreate experiences in their imaginations and identify the recognizable human experiences in the text. Resist the impulse to immediately reduce every biblical passage to a set of theological ideas. Let God speak to you through the passage. (Barclay [1972] 1997; ESV Study Bible 2011)

READING TO BE WITH GOD

In order to be with God, you must communicate with Him. Your primary source of communication with Him is prayer, which is the verbal aspect of your response to God in communion with Him. It is not optional, it is commanded (see Scripture #5). In prayer, God gets the glory, and you get the joy (see Scripture #6).

Scripture 5: **1 Thessalonians 5:17**

ESV	*Pray without ceasing.*
CSB	*Pray constantly.*
NIV	*Pray continually.*
NLT	*Never stop praying.*

Scripture 6: **John 16:24b**

ESV	*Ask, and you will receive, that your joy may be full.*
NLT	*Ask, using my name, and you will receive, and you will have abundant joy.*

Communion with God refers to His communication and presentation of Himself to you, together with your proper response to Him. God communicates with you in many ways throughout the

Bible. It is not merely learning about God. It is *enjoying a fellowship* with Him in the truth He reveals about Himself. (ESV Study Bible 2011)

The Bible records the deeds of God so that, by means of these, you have fellowship and communion with Him. The God-inspired record of history is the only infallible and authoritative book that communicates and presents God Himself. He is revealed by His Word. (ESV Study Bible 2011)

The message of how to be reconciled to God for the glory of God is the central message of the Bible. There is no communion with God without salvation from your sin and God's wrath.

What to Do and Where to Go?

So, you want to read the Bible, but you have no clue where to start. To start at the beginning can be daunting (have you **seen** Genesis?). Don't get me wrong, this is an acceptable plan. But, while some people do just start at the beginning and work through to the end, there are other options available that are less daunting.

READING PLANS

It is more beneficial to use a carefully prepared scheme of daily readings than to go it alone. Choosing a plan may take some time, but it will aid you in having a more focused time of reading. (Barclay [1972] 1997; Fairchild 2015a; Radiant Church 2015)

There are many types of reading plans. Just of few of those available are:

- beginning to end,
- chronological,
- OT, NT with Psalms and Proverbs,
- NT only, and
- NT with Psalms and Proverbs.

Plans also have different durations—from 90 days to one or two years. Since you can take any plan and adjust the duration of the reading time by adjusting how much you read each day, you should focus more on the order in which you want to read the Bible.

A few of the many sources available for finding a reading plan are:

- YouVersion (www.bible.com),
- Blue Letter Bible (www.blueletterbible.com),
- published Bible studies or devotionals,
- the website of your study Bible,
- your church library, or
- you can create your own.

Also, there are three plans contained on the Google drive (See Appendix A for URLs).

STUDYING

Studying the Bible is usually done topically. Let God lead you to the topic. He can bring you to it through different avenues (see Scripture #7). There are many topical studies already published. These will have comments and questions to help you get the most out of your study. (Virkler 2013)

Scripture 7: **John 16:13**

CSB	*When the Spirit of truth comes, he will guide you into all the truth. For he will not speak on his own, but he will speak whatever he hears. He will also declare to you what is to come.*
NIV	*But when he, the Spirit of truth, comes, he will guide you into all the truth. He will not speak on his own; he will speak only what he hears, and he will tell you what is yet to come.*
NLT	*When the Spirit of truth comes, he will guide you into all truth. He will not speak on his own but will tell you what he has heard. He will tell you about the future.*

You can, if you want, develop your own plan. To develop your own topical study, hit the concordance. Start with the verses listed under your topic and *SPIDER WEB* outward using the cross references in your Bible. If you use this method, you also should rely heavily on the commentaries that are available (especially through BLB).

REMEMBER

Things happen, **so be flexible in your plan** and be willing to make changes when necessary. You may find that the plan you have chosen isn't working for you. Drop it and choose another one. Perhaps the time you have chosen needs to be adjusted. Circumstances change. Don't be afraid to change with them. And, if you miss a day or two, do not stress out over it. Just pick up where you left off and continue your journey. (Fairchild 2015a)

Most importantly, be cleansed by His blood. Every time you sit down to be with the Lord, draw near to Him, repent of all sins, and ask for and receive the cleansing of His blood (see Scripture #8). In other words, pray. (Virkler 2013)

Scripture 8: **Hebrews 10:22**

ESV; CSB	Let us draw near with a true heart in full assurance of faith, with our hearts sprinkled clean from an evil conscience and our bodies washed with pure water.
NIV	Let us draw near to God with a sincere heart and with the full assurance that faith brings, having our hearts sprinkled to cleanse us from a guilty conscience and having our bodies washed with pure water.
NLT	Let us go right into the presence of God with sincere hearts fully trusting him. For our guilty consciences have been sprinkled with Christ's blood to make us clean, and our bodies have been washed with pure water.

Summary

In this chapter, you learned that what you get out of your Bible reading or study depends heavily on how you come to the Bible and what you put into it. This constitutes who you are as a person, and the attitude with which you approach your time with God as well as the effort you put into it.

There are many ways to approach the Bible. Your first decision is to decide if you are going to read it or study it. Often, both are done simultaneously. Reading and studying both involve multiple options for proceeding, so there are decisions to be made. Whatever you do, you need to do it on a regular basis—preferably daily.

The most important thing to consider is this: What is God telling you to do? He will place godly desires in your heart. So, what is on your heart to do?

Coming Attractions

The next three chapters discuss the nuts and bolts of reading or studying the Bible. Chapter six will focus on process, while chapters seven and eight will focus on understanding.

Points to Ponder

1. Write down the top two pieces of information from this chapter that were significant to you or surprised you the most. Explain why.

2. Of the items presented on how to come to the Bible, list the one you think is most important and discuss why.

5. You have decided to read the Bible. Develop a basic plan for doing so and list it here.

    Time of Day:

    How long each day:

    Over how many months:

    What obstacles do you foresee in activating this plan and how can they be overcome?

3. Compose a closing prayer asking God what He wants you to take away from this chapter. Then be still and listen. Write down whatever you think He is saying to you.

6

Step by Step by Step

Process for Reading or Studying the Bible

As previously mentioned, studying the Bible encompasses four processes: reading it, interpreting it, meditating on it, and teaching it. This chapter focuses on reading the Bible. Interpreting the Word and meditating on it will be talked about in chapters seven and eight. Chapter nine touches on sharing the Word, but an in-depth discussion of teaching is beyond the scope of this study. (Grace to You 2015)

Understand that Bible study begins with **actually reading Scripture**, not just books about the Bible or devotional materials based on it. That would be like trying to learn how ice cream tastes without eating any. You will never get the full flavor of it. (Grace to You 2015)

Prayer

Father God, as I study this chapter, open the eyes and ears of my spirit so that I can fully receive what You want me to know. Help me to take away from this chapter a better knowledge of how to study Your Word, as well as an increased hunger to do so. I ask this in Jesus' name, amen.

Chapter Verse: *Matthew 6:33*

CSB	*But seek first the kingdom of God and his righteousness, and all these things will be provided for you.*
NLT	*Seek the Kingdom of God above all else, and live righteously, and he will give you everything you need.*

Coming to Terms with Terms (Strong 1979; Kohlenberger 2015)

CELEBRATE: *(G2370 NIV)* To cause celebration, make glad; to celebrate, rejoice, be glad. *(G2165 Strong's)* To put in a good frame of mind, rejoice, make glad, be (make) merry, rejoice.

MEDITATION: *(H8488 NIV)* To meditate, muse on, consider, think on. *(H7878 Strong's)* To ponder, converse (with oneself, and hence aloud) or utter: commune, complain, declare, meditate, muse, pray, speak, talk (with).

SYNTHESIZING: The act of combining often-diverse concepts into a coherent whole; using deductive reasoning. Restating the concept in different words to clarify meaning.

WEEP: *(H1134 NIV)* To wail, cry, sob, mourn, to weep for, mourn for. This can refer to ritual mourning as well as personal sorrow. *(H1058 Strong's)* To weep, to bemoan, bewail, complain, make lamentation, mourn.

WORSHIP: *(H2556 NIV)* To bow down low (in worship); prostrate oneself; pay one honor, homage.
(H2331 Strong's) To live, to declare, or show.

How to Read/Study

The chapter verse commands you to seek God's Kingdom first. That may sound daunting at this point, but Proverbs 2:1-5 lays out how to do that (See Scripture #1).

Scripture 1: **Proverbs 2:1-5**

CSB	[1]*My son, if you accept my words and store up my commands within you,* [2]*listening closely to wisdom and directing your heart to understanding;* [3]*furthermore, if you call out to insight and lift your voice to understanding,* [4]*if you seek it like silver and search for it like hidden treasure,* [5]*then you will understand the fear of the LORD and discover the knowledge of God.*
NLT	[1]*My child, listen to what I say, and treasure my commands.* [2]*Tune your ears to wisdom, and concentrate on understanding.* [3]*Cry out for insight, and ask for understanding.* [4]*Search for them as you would for silver; seek them like hidden treasures.* [5]*Then you will understand what it means to fear the LORD, and you will gain knowledge of God.*

Detailed instructions for all of this will be covered in the next few chapters.

> To read the Bible with system and with help is the way to get the best out of it, for thus we will get strength for the way, wisdom for our minds, and the love of God for our hearts.
> —*William Barclay (Barclay [1972] 1997)*

> I study my Bible as I gather apples. First, I shake the whole tree that the ripest may fall. Then I shake each limb, and when I have shaken each limb, I shake every branch and every twig. Then I look under every leaf.
> —*Martin Luther (Bell & Campbell 2003)*

As you can see, the way to study is to be systematic while looking in every nook and cranny of the Bible to uncover all of God's truths. So, when you sit down to study, pray first. As you embark on your daily journey, pray for God to continue to fuel the desire and the discipline to spend time with him each day. Ask God to speak to you. Read for hearing not for speed, and read aloud—preferably with others—for deeper understanding. As you become more comfortable with Bible study, you will begin to develop your own techniques and discover favorite resources that will make your study very personal and meaningful. Respond with prayer when you are done for that session. (Barclay [1972] 1997; Bell & Campbell 2003; Fairchild 2015a; Fairchild 2015b; Radiant Church 2015)

The study of the Bible is not something that you will ever truly finish in your lifetime. There is always something else to discover in God's Word. However, the pursuit of that goal can be exhilarating, and it most definitely will be illuminating. When the grace and guidance of the Holy Spirit meet with your study and your toil, as well as the endeavor of your dedicated heart and mind, then, indeed, Scripture opens its riches. (Barclay [1972] 1997)

The Nuts and Bolts

The first rule of Bible study is that there are no hard and fast rules. No single plan fits all. In the same way that each person learns in his or her own style, no two people will have the exact same method of studying the Bible. There is no secret or *hack* on how to do it. (Stott 1999)

However, there are some guidelines that are a given and common to all plans: (Bell & Campbell 2003; Johnson 2003; Stott 1999)

- Bible study requires time to read and discover God's truth and then turn it over and over in your mind until it sinks into your heart.
- Time for reading or studying must be purposefully redeemed from your busy life. Most people discover that they have to schedule this time the same as any other appointment.
- There are general techniques, familiar to many:
  - Observe the facts of Scripture.
  - Interpret those facts in light of historical (cultural) and biblical (literary) context.
  - Determine ways to put it into practice in your life today.
- Bible study should be done every day.

The most difficult step is getting started. Everyone is busy, and the thought of adding another activity to an already-crowded agenda can be disheartening. It is hard wedging the time into your schedule to read your Bible every day. But what you get in return is priceless. It is well worth whatever wedging you need to do.

It is important to make the effort required to truly hear the Word and follow it. This calls for the hardest kind of thought, the most intense kind of study, the most strenuous exercise of reason in order to find the meaning of the words. Devotion will grasp the message of the Holy Spirit through grace, while scholarship will toil at the meaning of the words in which the message is expressed. Both approaches are valid and, really, intertwined. (Barclay [1972] 1997; Johnson 2003)

Come to your study with humility as well as with a teachable spirit. Ask the Holy Spirit to reveal His truth to you. Be willing to discover and embrace the truth, no matter how hard it is or what it costs. (Virkler 2013)

Logistics

KEY CONCEPT: The general framework for study includes praying, reading a Scripture passage (preferably aloud), meditating on it, praying about it, contemplating God in it, and determining how it applies to your life today. Most Bible study methods can be encompassed within this 30,000-foot-view of the process. (Johnson 2003)

PREPARATION

In general, there are four effective steps involved in preparing for your Bible study: 1) Purposefully set aside time. 2) Decide on a place. 3) Have all your materials available. 4) Prepare your heart. (Meyer 2015)

Set Aside Time

There is no right or wrong time of day to study the Bible; although, many people find that the first thing in the morning is best for two reasons. First, it is the only time of the day that they truly have control over, because once the day starts things can go awry very quickly. Second, and more importantly, it can give you the spiritual boost you need to carry you through the day. Just like you feed your body at similar times each day, spending time with God and feeding your spirit should be at similar times as well. Once determined, be intentional about guarding this time. You may need to let others in your circle know that this is your time with God, which is precious, and you don't want to be disturbed. (Fairchild 2015a)

You also must decide on a time frame for studying. Start with a realistic goal, such as 10 or 15 minutes. This can quickly develop into a longer span of time as you become engaged in your study. If you start with an unrealistic goal, like two hours, failure to meet the goal will soon discourage you and probably derail your Bible study efforts. (Fairchild 2015a)

Decide on a Place

Finding a place conducive to studying the Bible is a primary key to your success. The place you choose should be a specific place where you enjoy being and that is comfortable enough to make the experience enjoyable. Make sure it has a good light source and a place for all your study tools. But don't get too comfortable. Lying in bed with the lights low is a recipe for failure. Your personal study process will dictate some of the requirements of this place. For example, if you like to record what you learn in a computer document rather than with pen and paper, you will need a place that allows for the computer to be present. The place you choose also should be as free as possible of distractions. Studying the Bible while watching TV generally is not the most effective process. (Fairchild 2015a; Meyer 2015)

Just like with your time, your special study place needs to be guarded. Let those in your circle know that you don't want to be disturbed while you are there. (Fairchild 2015a)

Have All Your Materials Available

This process needs to be considered when deciding on a place for your Bible study. It sounds much easier than it is; something to record what you learn and your Bible, right? Let's see.

Accommodations

You absolutely do need your Bible, or Bibles as the case may be, and some medium for recording what you learn as well as for journaling. However, depending on how intensely you want to study, you also may want to have on hand a concordance, a Bible dictionary, a regular dictionary, a handbook of the Bible, or any other reference materials you find useful. You also will need access to whatever plan you are using to study the Bible—outline, study plan, or devotional materials.

Whatever materials that you choose to help you study the Bible, the space you choose should accommodate having all of them within reach from wherever you will sit during your study time. I don't think there is anything that interrupts the flow of the Holy Spirit during Bible study more than having to stop in order to get up and go retrieve something that you need.

What Structure?

Part of having all your materials available is deciding on what structure you will use in studying the Bible. Think of the structure as an outline or an agenda for a meeting. How much Bible reading will you do and in what order will you read it? How much time will you spend on devotional materials? How much time will you spend on a study guide? How much time in devotional conversation with God? (Fairchild 2015a)

There is no set rule on how much you should cover or even how long your daily sessions should be. In fact, this could be fluid from day to day depending on circumstances. But it is best to have some kind of plan going into it. Winging it is not very satisfying and can be quite frustrating. So, be a man (or woman) with a plan.

Prepare Your Heart

This step is done primarily in prayer. Ask God to examine your heart and let you know if there is anything there that will hinder the process of you hearing from God. If there is, you may have to repent before starting your study. (Meyer 2015)

Journaling

Keep a notebook, or a document on the computer, and record what you learn. This is called journaling and is a key aspect of studying the Bible. Recording what you discover binds the information to your mind in a way that merely listening, or reading does not. The more senses you engage during a study process, regardless of what you are studying, the better you retain the information. (Dekker 2016; Stott 2008)

Journaling should not be considered optional, but rather a vital part of your study process. The journal does not have to be extensive or detailed. It can be simple words or phrases that you jot down. However, be careful to write enough so that when you come back to it at a later date, it still makes sense to you. Your journal can even be pictures that you see if you are able to draw them. I have included *5 Prompts for Journaling Through Scripture* (Appendix D and Google drive at https://docs.google.com/document/d/1qS6PGVEh4DZHF4TS5ud1cTQ8MN-s7NS3aFWjYMN3WuE/copy) for additional information. (Crossway 2020, Fairchild 2015a)

By journaling your thoughts and prayers, as well as what God says to you, you are providing a valuable record of the things that God has shown you. It provides a resource for reference in the future. As you walk your journey with God, you will be surprised at how often you go back to previous journals for whatever reason. (Fairchild 2015a)

Be advised, journaling is not the same thing as note taking. In taking notes, you are writing down whatever strikes you, whatever is new to you, whatever tugs at your heart as you read. It is like taking notes in class. In journaling, you are *SYNTHESIZING* the information in your notes to determine what God is saying to you and how He wants you to apply it to your life. There are samples of journaling formats in Appendix C and on the Google drive (see Appendix A for individual links).

Down to the Nitty Gritty (Process)

There are several distinct steps to follow when reading the Bible: worship, opening prayer, reading the passage(s), studying the passage(s), and appropriate responses such as ending prayer, meditation, counsel. Each step is discussed in detail below.

WORSHIP

You should consider spending some time in *WORSHIP*. While it is not required, it can be extremely helpful in preparing your spirit to receive from God. There is no right or wrong way to worship. When most people hear the word *worship*, they think that means singing, but there are multiple ways to worship. Just standing and praising God with whatever words come to mind or using your prayer language is a form of worship. It is not required that the words be set to music. The key is focusing on God and, in some way, expressing your adoration and appreciation for His greatness, His love, His grace, and His mercy. (Fairchild 2015a)

BEGINNING PRAYER

As you can see from the list of citations at the end of the paragraph, virtually every source states that praying before you start to study is essential. Prayer and Bible study are two sides of the same coin. Before you start, ask God to give you openness and humility to hear what He is saying and to show you how the passage you are about to read fits into your life. (Barclay [1972] 1997; Fairchild 2015a; Fairchild 2015b; Johnson 2003; Radiant Church 2015; Stott 2008)

Remember that prayer is a two-way conversation. You ask, God answers, you respond, God answers, you respond, God answers …. The key is humility as well as an open mind and spirit to receive from God. (Johnson 2003)

> The first thing one needs to become a theologian through Bible reading is prayer for the illumination and help of the Holy Spirit.
> —*Martin Luther* (ESV Study Bible 2011)

READING

The first rule of reading is to set your own pace, but do not make that pace too fast. You need to read for understanding, not for speed. Careful students of Scripture will reread a passage, not only to find the main point of the passage, but to observe the way the biblical authors think. Read the passage a second (or third or fourth) time, preferably in different translations. Then read it slower, verse by verse, looking for a deeper understanding of what the author is saying. (ESV Study Bible 2011; Fairchild 2015b; Stott 2008)

Above all, whether reading or studying, ***look for Jesus in the text***. And, yes, this does apply to the Old Testament. Jesus is part of the entire Bible, not just the New Testament. (Stott 2008)

STUDYING

If your goal is just to read through the Bible, you can skip this step. Be aware that studying differs from reading. Studying is a process that takes you deeper into the passages or subject matter than reading does.

Genuine Bible study can occur in many ways. I am focusing on three different models for studying the Bible. Before I review the different models, there are some principals that apply to Bible study, regardless of the form it takes. (Johnson 2003)

First, do not be in a hurry when you study God's word. It took hundreds of years to write, it is going to take more than a minute to understand it. Next, ask God to answer some pertinent questions for you: What are the themes of the passage? What are the key words of the passage? What is the point of the passage? How do I apply this to my life? (Grace to You 2015)

STUDY METHODS

I have listed several different study methods that I found during my research. You can use any one of them, take certain parts from each one to create a unique design, or create your own method. Genuine study occurs in many ways, so there is no wrong way to study the Bible unless you are not hearing God's truth or growing in your relationship with Him. (Johnson 2003)

Questions to Ask
Whatever method you use to study the Bible, there are questions that you should be asking as you go. These fall into three primary areas: 1) the basic facts of the passage, 2) understanding the text, and 3) applying the passage to your life. These questions are not listed in any order of importance, because it is important to find the answers to all of them. (Johnson 2003)

Basic Facts
What does the passage say? Who is speaking? Who is being spoken to? What are the current circumstances?

Understanding the Text
What does the passage say about what God is like? What does it say about human nature? What does it say about how God relates to people?

Applying the Text
What does the passage suggest about how I might pray? What does it suggest about how I might act?

Study Method 1 (Fairchild 2015b; Radiant Church 2015)
1. Read the entire passage—book, chapter, verse(s). Take notes on ideas that jump out at you.
2. Read the passage a second time, preferably in a different translation.
3. If the passage is large enough (generally should be at least a chapter), outline it using natural, logical divisions.
   a. What are the themes of the passage? Write these in your own words using one sentence.
   b. What are the key words of the passage? Write them down (maybe under the theme).
4. Using a concordance or other study aide, look up the key words and find their definitions. You guessed it, write them down.
5. Reread the passage using the definitions. Does your stated theme change or expand?
6. Write a short synopsis in your own words of what the passage says and how you can apply it to your life today. This is journaling.

Study Method 2 (Johnson 2003)
1. Read the passage aloud. Watch for a word or phrase that emerges from the passage and stays with you, something that jumps off the page at you.
2. Determine what it is about that word or phrase that draws you.
3. Determine what God might be calling you to be through that word or phrase.
4. Pray and ask God why you are being drawn to that phrase. Is there something He might be calling you to do or something you should refrain from doing?
5. Quietly enjoy God's presence while you wait for the answer.
6. Determine in what situations or frames of mind it might be helpful to recall that word or phrase.
7. Journal your thoughts as well as what God says to you.

Study Method 3 (Johnson 2003)
1. Read the passage.
2. Dissect the passage.
   a. Ask questions about the passage.
   b. Read commentaries and study aides.
3. Compare the truths as well as new ways of applying those truths.
4. Journal your thoughts as well as what God says to you.

RESPONSES TO SCRIPTURE STUDY
We all have different responses when we study Scripture. These responses determine how much the words infiltrate our spirits. Five of the more common responses are discussed below. (Johnson 2003)

Meditation

MEDITATION is an active response. Today we associate meditation with the eastern version of being still and humming, inferring that it is a cerebral activity. But that is not the meaning of the original word. The original word encompassed verbal responses, mostly to ourselves, about what was studied. In our times this can be encompassed through journaling. (Kohlenberger 2015; Strong 1979)

Another part of meditation is to be fearless. Some churches have dire consequences for disagreeing with the church's beliefs. This hinders many from pursuing God's truth. As you meditate, put your whole trust in God first to show you the truth, and second to sustain you if that truth varies from what your church is teaching you (maybe time to find a new church?). It takes guts to stand up for God, but it is something that He rewards richly. (Virkler 2013)

Worshipping

God's word is so good that often our response is to worship him spontaneously. Again, this is not a cerebral response. Done wholeheartedly, it involves our entire spirit as well as our entire body. Those who worship fully before the Lord often are thought to be drunk. (Kohlenberger 2015; Strong 1979)

Celebrating

When you get good news, isn't your first reaction to CELEBRATE it? Well, there is no better news than the truths held in God's word. Therefore, celebrating God's word is a natural, as well as spiritual, reaction. Even the passages that are not so fun (such as those on tithing) are easier to absorb and put into action when we celebrate the truth within them. (Johnson 2003)

Weeping or Confessing Sin

This response encompasses being convicted by what you read to the point that you are brought, if not actually to physically WEEPING, then to a state where your spirit is weeping. It is recognizing that there is an area of your life that needs changing in order to fall in line with God's precepts and the conviction that it brings. With conviction comes sorrow. Hopefully, with all this comes a confession of your sin and an expression of regret for having committed, or lived in a state of, sin as well as a promise to do better (repentance). This can be a powerful, cleansing action that, usually, will bring with it celebration. (Johnson 2003)

Praying

If your time with God is spent earnestly, prayer is a natural response following study. Talk to God about what He is talking to you about. Simply have a conversation with Him. Thank Him for any insights or revelations He has provided during your time together. Possibly use what He has taught you in future prayers.

> When in reading Scripture you meet with a passage that seems to give your heart a new motion toward God, turn it into the form of a petition, and give it a place in your prayers.
> —*William Law* (Johnson 2003)

Summary

This chapter talked about the nitty gritty of Bible study. It explained the overall process as well as provided several different study methods to use as a reference for developing your own method. While no two people study the Bible exactly the same, prayer and journaling should be part of everyone's process. It is important that you begin and end with prayer. Ask God to open your spiritual senses before you begin. Then thank Him for what He has shown you when you are done. Record everything He says to you during the session.

Coming Attractions

In chapter seven you will learn about interpreting what you read in the Bible. While there are entire college courses on this topic, I will break it down to the essentials that you need to be aware of as you read or study God's Word.

Points to Ponder

1. Write down the top two pieces of information from this chapter that were significant to you or surprised you the most. Explain why.

2. After reading this chapter, would you change anything about the plan you listed in chapter 5? If so, write down your new plan. List all the steps.

3. Of the five responses to Scripture listed in the text, which have you experienced in the past? Which one would you like to try more often? Why?

4. Compose a closing prayer asking God what He wants you to take away from this chapter. Then be still and listen. Write down whatever you think He is saying to you.

7

What on Earth Does That Mean?

Interpretation of the Bible

In this chapter you will be shown how to interpret and understand what you read in the Bible. The topic is so large and complex that there are several college courses on how to do this. However, by the time you have completed chapters 7 and 8, you will have a basic understanding of the process.

Prayer

Father God, thank you for your pull on my life to know you better. As I study how to interpret Your Word, I ask that the Holy Spirit open up all my spiritual senses as well as infuse me with a spirit of understanding so that I may glean all that You want me to know about interpreting Your Word. I ask this in Jesus' name, amen.

Chapter Verse: *Isaiah 11:2, 9b*

CSB	*² The Spirit of the LORD will rest on him—a Spirit of wisdom and understanding, a Spirit of counsel and strength, a Spirit of knowledge and of the fear of the LORD. ⁹ ... for the land will be as full of the knowledge of the LORD as the sea is filled with water.*
NLT	*²And the Spirit of the LORD will rest on him—the Spirit of wisdom and understanding, the Spirit of counsel and might, the Spirit of knowledge and the fear of the LORD. ⁹... for as the waters fill the sea, so the earth will be filled with people who know the LORD.*

Coming to Terms with Terms

ALLEGORICAL: A representation that is symbolic.

ANAGOGICAL: Interpretation of a word, passage, or text (such as Scripture or poetry) that finds beyond the literal, allegorical, and moral senses; a fourth and ultimate spiritual or mystical sense.

APOCALYPTIC: Something viewed as a prophetic revelation, often using symbolic or figurative language.

EXEGESIS: What does it say? The careful, systematic study of Scripture to discover the original, intended meaning.

GENRE: A category of artistic, musical, or literary composition characterized by a particular style, form, or content.

HERMENEUTICS: What does it mean? Hearing the text of Scripture in relation to what it means, and how we apply it, today.

LITERAL: In accordance with the letter of the Scriptures; adhering to fact or to the ordinary construction or primary meaning of a term or expression.

MORAL: Of or relating to principles of right and wrong in behavior.

The Big Words

EXEGESIS? HERMENEUTICS? Say what? Don't panic. The sole purpose of this section is to introduce two of the most commonly used terms when reading various reference materials about studying or interpreting the Bible.

EXEGESIS is a big word that means finding out what the author originally said. What did the words mean then? What do they mean now?

HERMENEUTICS is another big word that means to figure out what the passage means to us today. How does it apply to today's society? How does it apply to me? What am I supposed to do with it?

So, simply put, exegesis is another word for understanding and hermeneutics is another word for finding application for your life.

Interpretation

Overview

You hear the word interpretation, and you panic. Don't. You do not need to be a scholar to interpret the Bible, you just need to ask the right questions, which are discussed in more detail later. The aim of any good interpretation is to get at the plain meaning of the text, which requires work. (Fee & Stuart 2014; Grace to You 2015)

The Bible was written in three different languages. Most of the OT was written in Hebrew while half of Daniel and all of Ezra are in Aramaic, which is a sister language to Hebrew. The NT was written in Koine Greek, the common language of the day. (Bell & Campbell 2003; Fee & Stuart 2014)

As you are interpreting the Scriptures, remember that the main point of the passage should not necessarily be considered the only point or even the key point. God has many layers. So does His word. You need to look at the matter in light of the whole mind and character of Jesus Christ as you know them, as well as in the light of the mind and heart of God. Compare your interpretation with the totality of Scripture, because all Scripture fits together. The Bible does not contradict itself. (Barclay [1972] 1997; ESV Study Bible 2011; Grace to You 2015)

Also keep in mind that the OT is promise, a promise of things to come, of what God is going to do. The NT is fulfillment; fulfillment of the promises given in the OT, fulfillment in the person of Jesus Christ. Your interpretation needs to lead beyond a conceptual knowledge of the Word to the person of Jesus Christ as well as to a vital relationship with Him. (ESV Study Bible 2011; Stott 1999)

Finally, you need to make use of all the aids that the Lord sets before you for the understanding of Scripture. There are, of course, all the tools of the trade listed in chapter four. However, God has provided us with three other sources of wisdom—the Holy Spirit, yourself, and your church family. The roles of the Holy Spirit and yourself will be discussed later. (Stott 1999)

The Church is a valuable source of instruction. God does not give His knowledge to only a select few. He gives it to everyone who is righteous—right with God—and who seeks Him. Knowing this, you need to be willing to listen to, and learn from, others. You also need to be willing to teach others. Our minds are illumined through group study as well as individual study. Both are important. (Stott 1999)

What Is Interpretation?

You wonder why you need to know about interpretation because, after all, you are "just reading" the Bible. It is because everybody interprets **anything** they read based on experiences, culture, and prior knowledge. Fee and Stuart (2014) give a good example in their book based on Romans 13:14 (see Scripture #1). When most people read *flesh*, they translate that to mean the *body*. However, the intention Paul had was more along the lines of *sinful nature*.

Scripture 1: Romans 13:14

CSB	But put on the Lord Jesus Christ, and don't make plans to gratify the desires of the flesh.
NLT	Instead, clothe yourself with the presence of the Lord Jesus Christ. And don't let yourself think about ways to indulge your evil desires.

Translators need to make decisions about these kinds of apparent contradictions. The primary decision is whether they translate the word as flesh, which is the dictionary meaning, or do they translate it as evil desires or sinful nature, which is the intended meaning? Thus, the differences in the various Bible translations, as shown in Scripture 1. As you can see, interpretation of the Bible is an art as well as a spiritual task. (ESV Study Bible 2011; Fee & Stuart 2014)

While there is generally only one true interpretation of a passage, there are many possible applications. Once you read the passage and know what it says, the next step is to find out what it means. Scholars of the Middle Ages spoke of a fourfold meaning, or sense, of Scripture. (1) The *LITERAL* sense tells what happened. (2) The *ALLEGORICAL* sense tells what you are to believe. (3) The *MORAL* sense tells what you are to do. (4) The *ANAGOGICAL* sense tells what you may hope for. (Barclay [1972] 1997; ESV Study Bible 2011; Grace to You 2015)

> The true meaning of the biblical text for us is what God originally intended it to mean
> when it was first spoken or written.
> —*Gordon D. Fee and Douglas Stuart (Fee & Stuart 2014)*

The starting point for all biblical interpretation must be the attempt to find out what the writer intended, because a text cannot mean something other than what it meant for its original readers and hearers. However, the original meaning must be put into the context of today. The concern of the scholar is what the passage meant when it was written. The concern of the layperson is what it means today. Most will agree that we need some of both for proper perspective. (Barclay [1972] 1997; Fee & Stuart 2014)

Issues of Interpretation

Throughout time, getting people to come into agreement about what the Bible means has been a very challenging task. We are taught to get at the *plain meaning* of the text. However, that is not the same for everybody. For some it may be what the interpreter wants it to say in order to support his or her hypothesis or point of view. **Do not make this mistake**. Avoid making the Bible say just what you want it to say. While most people may agree that the Bible is a divinely inspired and essential religious text, not everyone will arrive at the same conclusions about its teachings. (Bell & Campbell 2003; Fee & Stuart 2014; Grace to You 2015)

When both sides of a topic or debate can cite the Bible as their authority to support their point of view, it is not easy to reach an agreement. When this happens, it is reasonable to assume that more careful study needs to be done by both sides on both references, because the Bible never contradicts itself. Chances are that the passages have been taken out of context, and the context is critical to proper understanding. (Bell & Campbell 2003)

Among believers, all will agree that the Bible provides God's truth for our lives, but how to interpret that truth is another question. For example, consider the story of the five blind men who examined the elephant; each was completely convinced that he had the correct perception. The elephant, indeed, was much like a tree (around the leg), a rope (at the tail), a fan (at the ear), a hose (at the trunk) and a wall (on the side). Each man was absolutely correct in the extent of his knowledge. The problem was that none of them had grasped the animal in its entirety. Instead of discussing and comparing notes using what little they *did* know to get a better picture, they preferred to argue about who was right. (Bell & Campbell 2003)

The issue of language is a huge one. You are told that you need to understand the language of the Bible. Unfortunately, people vary in their opinions of what is to be taken literally and what is figurative or symbolic. Each person tends to draw those lines in separate places, and it's not as simple as one is right, and one is wrong. There are differences even in the various translations. The meanings of the words, grammatical relationships in sentences, and choices in translation of the original texts are where they differ. This is because much of the original language cannot be translated directly into today's languages. (Bell & Campbell 2003; Fee & Stuart 2014; Stott 1999)

However long and devotedly you study the Bible, no matter how many resources you use, there still will be passages that are difficult and that you are unable to understand at this time. Spiritual revelation is an ongoing process. God offers the blaze of truth at all time, but the mind of man is capable of, and willing to, receive only a limited amount of it at any given time. When you find a passage you cannot understand, leave it and move on. The day may come when you will understand it. (Barclay [1972] 1997)

Principles of Interpretation

There are three primary principles of interpretation: simplicity, history, and harmony.

THE PRINCIPLE OF SIMPLICITY is where you look for the *natural* sense of the biblical text. Keep in mind that, sometimes, the natural meaning is figurative rather than literal. God's whole purpose in speaking and in causing his speech to be preserved is that he wanted to communicate to ordinary people (just like you and me) and save them. (Stott 1999)

THE PRINCIPLE OF HISTORY is where you look for the *original* sense of Scripture. The permanent and universal message of Scripture can be understood only in the light of the circumstances in which it was originally given. (Stott 1999)

THE PRINCIPLE OF HARMONY is where you look for the *general* sense of Scripture. It is important to learn to see the Bible as a whole, and to read each passage in the light of its entirety. Harmony does not deny that there has been progression in God's revelation of Himself and of His purposes. Rather, it emphasizes that the progression has not been from error to truth, but from truth to more truth. (Stott 1999)

Role of the Holy Spirit (and Yourself)

Our foremost teacher is the Holy Spirit. This same Spirit, who moved the writers of the Bible, is the Spirit who now enables you to study and interpret these books. His objective is two-fold. First there is the objective stage of disclosure (information), which is the stating of truth. Then there is the subjective stage of illumination (understanding), which is enlightenment of your mind, so you can comprehend the truth. He informs you of His truth—what it is. Then he illuminates His truth—what it means to you. The Lord will not allow you to labor in vain. If you show that you are not teachable, He can make you teachable. Once you are teachable, He will teach you. (Barclay [1972] 1997; Stott 1999)

If the Holy Spirit is your first teacher, you, in your dependence on the Spirit, must also teach yourself. You are expected to use your own reasoning ability responsibly. See Scripture #2. (Stott 1999)

Scripture 2: **Luke 12:57; 1 Corinthians 10:15**

ESV	*Luke 12:57 And why do you not judge for yourselves what is right?* *1 Corinthians 10:15 I speak as to sensible people; judge for yourselves what I say.*
NLT	*Luke 12:57 Why can't you decide for yourselves what is right?* *1 Corinthians 10:15 You are reasonable people. Decide for yourselves if what I am saying is true.*

Role of Christ

The authors of the Bible were not writing history. The primary aim of these chosen people was to show God in action. Your primary purpose in reading or studying the Bible is to determine where Jesus appears in the midst of each passage. Every verse in the Bible points to Jesus in some way. Your goal is to decipher what each passage has to do with Him.

Context

As you read or study the Bible, you must do so with awareness of the contexts. There are two aspects for every context: (1) historical, i.e., what the setting was, and (2) literary, i.e., what the occasion and purpose was. A part of the literary context is the content, or what is being said. For this, a knowledge of the genres of the Bible, and how to interpret them, is necessary (See chapter 2). (ESV Study Bible 2011; Fee & Stuart 2014)

It is important to know who the writer is as well as who and what he or she represented at the time of writing. God made full use of the personality, temperament, background, and experience of the biblical writers in order to convey through each an appropriate and distinctive message. Here are seven examples: Amos = prophet of God's justice; Hosea = love; Isaiah = kingly sovereignty; Paul = grace and faith; James = works; John = love; and Peter = hope. (Stott 1999)

Cultural

It is important to understand the culture of the time in which the passage was written. If you don't, you will never understand its meaning. One of the issues related to the culture of that time is that some of the instructions given to the people of that day tend not to be translated clearly across the centuries. (Bell & Campbell 2003; Grace to You 2015; Stott 1999;)

Since culture is part of the larger topic of history, knowing the historical background of the text also enriches your understanding. Historical context includes acknowledgement of the culture, as well as the economy, geography, climate, agriculture, architecture, family life, morals, and social structure of the Bible's writers, actors, and readers. God's truths have been made known in and through the living experience of human beings. For example, *whole world*, in biblical times, may have been limited to simply the middle east. Today it encompasses a *lot* more geography. (ESV Study Bible 2011; Grace to You 2015; Stott 1999)

This may sound daunting, but if you are able to obtain a good study Bible, the extra articles and introductions to each chapter will enlighten you to most of this information. What is not found in the chapter introductions, you probably can find in the notes for each verse.

Literary

Literary context includes the words, sentences, and paragraphs preceding and following a passage. There is a hierarchy to studying the Bible. Words only have meaning in sentences, and biblical sentences have full and clear meaning only in relation to preceding and succeeding sentences. (ESV Study Bible 2011; Fee & Stuart 2014)

Whatever means of communication God employed with the writers of the Bible, it never overpowered their own personality. As they wrote, their literary style and vocabulary were their own. That is why it is important to understand the style or literary genre of the passage. (Stott 1999)

READING THE DIFFERENT GENRES

The most customary way to define any literature is by the external genre. There are many forms of communication used in the Bible. Each form is considered a genre. See chapter two for a list of the primary genres appearing in the Bible. (ESV Study Bible 2011; Fee & Stuart 2014)

The genre of the passage being read should be noted since each genre has a distinct mode of operation. Additionally, many of the genres have subtypes within them. It is important to learn the rules of each genre. (ESV Study Bible 2011; Fee & Stuart 2014;)

Old Testament

There are three primary genres in the OT: Law, Writings, and Prophecy. Each of these has sub-genres, as was exhibited in *Table 1* of chapter two. However, many consider the OT to be a work of prophecy in the broadest sense of the term. It is a prophetic interpretation—because the word comes from God—of the events of Israel's history. In these Scriptures, God is revealed through the way the events are narrated.

Law

The genre of law constitutes the first five books of the Bible. They lay out everything from the beginning of the world ("In the beginning. . .") to the commandments to the genealogy of God's chosen people to the complete history of the Israelites until they reach the promised land. The primary sub-genre is history.

Prophecy

The prophetic books record the words that God gave to His chosen prophets. These people held the office of prophet. While the prophetic books center on God's prophets, they are not the only prophetic parts of the Bible. Many of the writings have a sub-genre of prophecy.

God tells us that all may prophesy (see Scripture #3). As such, there are sections of the writings where God bestowed prophetic words upon the writers of those books.

Scripture 3: Joel 2:28

CSB	*After this I will pour out my Spirit on all humanity; then your sons and your daughters will prophesy, your old men will have dreams, and your young men will see visions.*
NLT	*Then, after doing all those things, I will pour out my Spirit upon all people. Your sons and daughters will prophesy. Your old men will dream dreams, and your young men will see visions.*

Writings

The genres of law and prophecy are pretty straightforward, presenting a fairly unified, homogeneous group. This is not so with the writings. The writings are a miscellaneous collection that constitute the religious literature of a nation. (Barclay [1972] 1997)

New Testament

The NT consists of the Gospels and the Epistles along with Acts and Revelation, which are considered their own genres.

Gospels

The Gospels, while appearing to be historical, are not intended to be biographies of Jesus. That is why the order of events is not consistent throughout all four books. They are the preaching material of the early church. They show the mind, heart, and character of Jesus so that those who read them may see the mind, heart, and character of God in Jesus. The Gospels are an invitation from God to believe in Jesus as the Son of God. (Barclay [1972] 1997)

Epistles

The Epistles—or letters—all stem from the first century. They are not at all homogeneous. Some of them are intended for a specific person, while some are intended for public enlightenment. They are all occasional documents, that is, arising out of, and intended for, a specific occasion or need. They are, in essence, applied theology. (Fee & Stuart 2014)

Acts

Acts has been regarded as the history of the early church. It is not. The Scripture in Acts opens a series of windows through which we are shown remarkable events in the history of the early Church. The Book of Acts accomplishes three things: (Barclay [1972] 1997)

- It tells the story of the expansion of the Church.
- It tells how this astonishing crusade began with no more than 120 people and how it was the Word of the Holy Spirit.
- It tells us the message of the early church (all of which is pertinent to our lives today).

Revelation

Revelation is considered an *APOCALYPTIC* book. It is a recording of the prophecy that God gave to John. Because of the content of Revelation, people often correlate apocalyptic with disaster on the grandest scale. However, when Biblical commentators speak of apocalyptic writings, they are speaking about works that were written in a style similar to the book of Revelation—writings that employ symbolic or figurative language to describe a future divine intervention. (Butler 2003)

Immersion

Think of Bible study as an immersion into God's counsel for living wisely (see Scripture #4). (Johnson 2003)

Scripture 4: Deuteronomy 6:6

ESV	And these words that I command you today shall be on your heart.
CSB; NIV	These words that I am giving you today are to be in your heart.
NLT	And you must commit yourselves wholeheartedly to these commands that I am giving you today.

> It is necessary to immerse ourselves in [the Bible], to let it permeate our flesh, to grow so familiar with it that we possess it in the depths of our being and hold it in our memory.
> —Enzo Bianchi (Johnson 2003)

Enter into the world of the Bible the same as you would the world of a novel, as if you were there. Incorporate all five of your natural senses and use your imagination to enter the biblical scene as an observer. Imagine what you would see, hear, smell, touch or taste if you were present in the biblical scene. As you do this, one of the most important things to remember is that it contradicts and challenges your own world, the one that you are in, but not of. (Barclay [1972] 1997; ESV Study Bible 2011; Johnson 2003).

The Investigative Process

To understand any book, you must try to enter into the mind, the heart, the life, and the circumstances of the writer. It is here that you become like an investigative reporter, searching out the who, what, when, where, why, and how of the passage. (Barclay [1972] 1997)

WHO is writing the passage? Who is the author writing to?

WHAT happens in previous and succeeding passages? What is the symbolism of items mentioned in the passage as well as the whole of Scripture? What are the circumstances of the writer? What are the circumstances of the subjects or recipients of the passage? What does the passage say? What does the passage mean?

WHEN did it take place? (To answer this, use a good study Bible or a Bible dictionary).

WHERE are they? Where is the writer? Where are the subjects or recipients?

WHY is the author writing the passage? Why is it important? Why did God include this in His Word?

HOW does God reveal Himself in the passage? How does this passage reveal Christ? How does God fulfill His covenant promises in the passage?

Answering these questions will take you a long way down the road to understanding what God is saying to you and what the passage means for your life.

Summary

This chapter showed you the importance of interpreting what you read in the Bible as well as guidelines for doing so. It gave you various techniques to use to help you understand what you read.

Coming Attractions

The next chapter will discuss what to do with what you read. It will talk about how to make God's Word your own. The chapter has been kept short because you will be assigned a mini study to do on your own.

Points to Ponder

1. Write down the top two pieces of information from this chapter that were significant to you, or surprised you the most. Explain why.

2. In your own words, explain what interpretation is as it relates to Bible study.

3. List at least three issues with interpretation and why you need to be aware of them.

4. Compose a closing prayer asking God what He wants you to take away from this chapter. Then be still and listen. Write down whatever you think He is saying to you.

8

What Now Coach?

What to Do with What You Read

In chapter seven you learned how to interpret what you read in the Bible, so you can gain an understanding of what God is saying. In this chapter, you will learn what to do with what you have read and what you have heard from God. You will learn how to process it and be given practical steps for applying God's word to your own life.

This chapter was kept short specifically to allow you extra time this week to work on the mini study that you will be assigned.

Prayer

Thank You, Father, for continuing to feed my desire to know You better. As I study this chapter, Holy Spirit, open the eyes and ears of my spirit so that I can see and hear clearly what You are saying to me. Lord, help me to fully understand what to do to follow-up on the Scripture I read and study so that it becomes part of my spirit and my life. I ask this in the name of Jesus. Amen.

Chapter Verse: *James 1:22*

ESV; CSV	*But be doers of the word, and not hearers only, deceiving yourselves.*
NIV	*Do not merely listen to the word, and so deceive yourselves. Do what it says.*
NLT	*But don't just listen to God's word. You must do what it says. Otherwise, you are only fooling yourselves.*

Coming to Terms with Terms

CULTURAL TRANSPOSITION:	The practice of transposing the teaching of Scripture from one culture into another.
SYNTHESIZING:	The act of combining often-diverse concepts into a coherent whole; using deductive reasoning. Restating the concept in different words to clarify meaning.

Digesting the Word

So, you have studied the passage. "What now?" you ask. There are four steps remaining that you should work through in order to help what you have read or studied seep into your spirit: meditation, *SYNTHESIZING*, journaling, and application, each of which is discussed below.

Meditation

WHAT IT IS

Meditation, at its core, is talking to yourself about God. It is:

- the process that molds the individual parts of Scripture into a cohesive comprehension of biblical truth,
- another word for deep thinking and reflection, and
- God's Spirit utilizing every faculty of your heart and mind to bring forth revelation, which ushers in transformation. (Biblica.com 2014; Radiant Church 2015; Virkler 2013)

> It is not that you will think about what you have read, but you will feed upon what you have read. Out of a love for the Lord you exert your will to hold your mind quiet before Him. In this peaceful state, swallow what you have tasted, take in what is there as nourishment.
> —Jeanne Guyon (Johnson 2003)

WHY WE DO IT

The Bible commands us to meditate (see Scripture #1). In the King James version, we are told to attend to His word. Other translations say to pay attention. In any case, we are to give some time to God's words. To attend to the Word of God is a lot more than just reading, it is meditating on it. So, meditate on what you read. Allow it to marinate in your spirit. Let God speak into your life. (Meyer 2015; Radiant Church 2015)

Scripture 1: Proverbs 4:20-21

KJV	[20]My son, attend to my words; incline thine ear unto my sayings. [21]Let them not depart from thine eyes; keep them in the midst of thine heart.
CSB	[20]My son, pay attention to my words; listen closely to my sayings. [21]Don't lose sight of them; keep them within your heart.
NLT	[20]My child, pay attention to what I say. Listen carefully to my words. [21]Don't lose sight of them. Let them penetrate deep into your heart,

RESULTS OF MEDITATION

The *NIV Life Application Study Bible* (2011) states in the notes for Psalm 1:2 (see Scripture #2) that you can learn how to follow God through meditating on His Word; that knowing and meditating on God's Word are the first steps toward applying it to your everyday life. If you want to follow God more closely, you need to know what He says.

Scripture 2: Psalm 1:2

CSB	Instead, his delight is in the LORD's instruction, and he meditates on it day and night.
NIV	But whose delight is in the law of the LORD, and who meditates on his law day and night.
NLT	But they delight in the law of the LORD, meditating on it day and night.

You should repeatedly meditate and reflect on Scripture, because reading or studying it is not enough. The one who meditates on what he or she reads becomes the one who obeys, who is careful to follow God's word. Through meditation, your connection with God is extended and made stronger. When you discover and dig up a Scriptural treasure on your own, you take ownership of it at a much deeper level. (Biblica.com 2014; Dekker 2016; Johnson 2003)

To know a fact or truth in your mind (information) does not mean you believe in it enough that your behavior changes (understanding). Since understanding promotes transformation, you should meditate frequently, especially in the areas where you are seeking change. (Johnson 2003; Virkler 2013)

MEDITATION STYLES

As with learning styles, meditation styles vary from person to person. Below is a list of several styles. Consider which one(s) might best fit with the way you process life: (Johnson 2003)

- Soaking in and absorbing the meanings of words.

- Looking for a word or phrase that speaks to you.
- Picturing the ideas expressed or scenes described in the passage.
- Enjoying how words are combined—such as obedience and meditation—and *connecting the dots* between these ideas.
- Personalizing words of Scripture with specifics by inserting your own everyday activities or common sins into the text.
- Reading the passage aloud and simply resting or waiting to hear from God; waiting for a word or phrase to resonate.

Mark Virkler (2013) has a 7-step process for meditating. The complete article, which appears on the Internet, is on the Google drive (See Appendix A for URL). In a nutshell: become still in God's presence, possibly with soaking music in the background; picture yourself in a scene with God, then ask the Lord what He wants to show you about the passage; accept God's revelation, speak it forth, and act. The last step may require confessing and repenting of sin.

Synthesizing

The goal of SYNTHESIZING is to take what you have read and put it into your own words. It is important to find for yourself the will of God. It also is good practice to do this before you begin using your study tools. That gives God's Word an opportunity to speak to you personally. Pull out themes, revelations, and applications; then write them down. After you have done this, refer to your study aides to see what others have said. Once you have found the will of God in the passage, you should not only know it, but obey it. (Barclay [1972] 1997; Fairchild 2015b; Fee & Stuart 2014)

Journaling

This topic was covered in chapter six. This is simply a reminder of the importance of this activity. So, keep a notebook or a computer document and record what you learn. (Stott 2008)

Practical Application

The study of Scripture is meant to lead to action. Jesus teaches a parable (Matthew 13:3-9 and Mark 4:3-8) about a farmer who sows seeds that fall on various kinds of soil, each of which produces a different result (see Appendix E). The URL for the Google drive document is found in *URLs for Websites and Supplemental Resources* in Appendix A. The good news is you can change your soil, and thus your spiritual results, through proper application of the principles in God's Word. All of God's promises are if-then situations. You must do your part (the *if* part) before God can do His part (the *then* part). (Barclay [1972] 1997)

> Happy is he, then, who reads the Scriptures, if he converts the words into actions.
> —*Aelfric (early translator of the Bible)* (Barclay [1972] 1997)

MEANING OF APPLICATION

Application is using the instructions found in the Bible to walk out in your life. It starts with your complete honesty about where you need help. It is a lifelong process where you continually seek to expand and deepen your wisdom. Primary prerequisites for biblical application are careful prayer and meditation. However, it is important to realize that application is more than just following commands. Applying Scripture to your life means accepting and fulfilling God-given duties, seeking a godly character, pursuing goals that the Lord blesses, and seeing the world His way. (ESV Study Bible 2011; Radiant Church 2015)

It is not the regulations of a book with which you are dealing; it is the commands of the person, Jesus Christ, who spoke only truth. Truth is something to be done, not merely known (see the chapter verse). God's purpose in and through the Bible is relentlessly high; it is to change your life to bring you closer to Him. Thus, a study of the Bible should lead beyond conceptual knowledge to the Person of Jesus Christ, and a vital relationship with Him. (Barclay [1972] 1997; ESV Study Bible 2011; Stott 1999)

LISTENING

The foundation of application is attentively listening to what God says. One of God's recurring complaints in the biblical record itself is that His people continually turned a deaf ear to His Word. When you study a passage, it becomes your own only when you listen to what God is saying to you and then accept it into your spirit. (ESV Study Bible 2011)

You should discover for yourself the will of God through listening. The Holy Spirit answers prayer by giving discernment to understand and apply Scripture to your own situation. Those who seek will find. Again, once you have found it, you should not just know it, you should also obey it. (Barclay [1972] 1997; ESV Study Bible 2011)

As important as it is, listening to God's voice, and knowing His truths are not enough. You are blessed only when you apply them to your life. (Stott 1999)

ACCEPTANCE AND WISDOM

ACCEPTANCE: Remember the parable of the sower (see Appendix E). The different soils mentioned represent the varying levels of **reception** which people give God's word. You can change your soil through reception. Really there are only two possible attitudes to God's Word: either you receive it, or you reject it. Which one do you think is more beneficial? (Stott 1999)

WISDOM: God reveals Himself and His purposes throughout Scripture. Wise application always starts there, in His Word. There is wisdom to be found even in the parts of Scripture that you are not so fond of. One of the things most people groan about is all the lists in the Bible. But those lists have purpose and contain wisdom. Consider all these things that are communicated through His lists. (ESV Study Bible 2011)

- The Lord writes down names in His book of life.
- Families and communities matter to him.
- God is faithful to His promises throughout our long history.
- He enlists His people as troops in the redemptive reconquest of a world gone bad.
- All the promises of God find their *yes* in the person of Jesus Christ.

RATIONALE

The Bible repeatedly affirms that the words are written for us (you and me). See Deuteronomy 29:29; Romans 14:4; 1 Corinthians 10:11; and 2 Timothy 3:15-17. Your constant challenge is to reapply Scripture in a new way, because God's purpose is always to rescript your life. In doing so, it is important to recognize that biblical instruction itself is permanently binding, but also that it needs to be translated into contemporary cultural terms to apply it. This is called CULTURAL TRANSPOSITION and it is essential to recognize that its purpose is not to avoid obedience, but, rather, to ensure it, by making it contemporary, making it relevant to today. (ESV Study Bible 2011; Stott 1999)

PROCESS

"So how do I do that?" you ask. As with studying, there is no one perfect process. You were previously told that you are called to be a doer of the word, which means practice what you have read. John Stott lists five avenues to application: worship (see Scripture #4), repentance (see Scripture #5), faith (see Scripture #6), obedience (see Scripture #7), and witness (see Scripture #8). (Fairchild 2015b; Radiant Church 2015; Stott 1999)

Scripture 4: Psalm 148:13 *(Worship)*

CSB	Let them praise the name of the LORD, for his name alone is exalted. His majesty covers heaven and earth.
NIV	Let them praise the name of the LORD, for his name alone is exalted; his splendor is above the earth and the heavens.
NLT	Let them all praise the name of the LORD. For his name is very great; his glory towers over the earth and heaven!

Scripture 5: **Jeremiah 7:3** *(Repentance)*

ESV	*Thus, says the LORD of hosts, the God of Israel: Amend your ways and your deeds, and I will let you dwell in this place.*
CSB	*This is what the LORD of Armies, the God of Israel, says: Correct your ways and your actions, and I will allow you to live in this place.*
NIV	*This is what the LORD Almighty, the God of Israel, says: Reform your ways and your actions, and I will let you live in this place.*

Scripture 6: **Hebrews 11:6** *(Faith)*

CSB	*Now without faith it is impossible to please God, since the one who draws near to him must believe that he exists and that he rewards those who seek him.*
NIV	*And without faith it is impossible to please God, because anyone who comes to him must believe that he exists and that he rewards those who earnestly seek him.*
NLT	*And it is impossible to please God without faith. Anyone who wants to come to him must believe that God exists and that he rewards those who sincerely seek him.*

Scripture 7: **John 14:15, 21** *(Obedience)*

ESV	*15"If you love me, obey my commandments. ... 21Those who accept my commandments and obey them are the ones who love me. And because they love me, my Father will love them. And I will love them and reveal myself to each of them."*
CSB	*15"If you love me, you will keep my commands. ... 21"The one who has my commands and keeps them is the one who loves me. And the one who loves me will be loved by my Father. I also will love him and will reveal myself to him."*
NLT	*15"If you love me, obey my commandments. ... 21Those who accept my commandments and obey them are the ones who love me. And because they love me, my Father will love them. And I will love them and reveal myself to each of them."*

Scripture 8: **Acts 4:33** *(Witness)*

CSB	*With great power the apostles were giving testimony to the resurrection of the Lord Jesus, and great grace was on all of them.*
NIV	*With great power the apostles continued to testify to the resurrection of the Lord Jesus. And God's grace was so powerfully at work in them all.*
NLT	*The apostles testified powerfully to the resurrection of the Lord Jesus, and God's great blessing was upon them all.*

God does the applying of the truths. Your life and God's Word meet. He awakens your sense of need, gives you ears to hear, and freely gives necessary wisdom. The passage and your life become fused. (ESV Study Bible 2011)

Look for directly applicable passages, passages that are obvious in what God is asking you to do. The application of your favorite passages usually is quite straightforward. Tackle these first. (ESV Study Bible 2011)

While reading, recognize the sorts of passages where personal application is less direct. You need to tackle these, also, but they require more effort. The Bible's stories, histories, and prophecies—even many of the commands, teachings, promises, and prayers—take thoughtful work and meditation in order to apply them to your life with current relevance. (ESV Study Bible 2011)

Whatever passage you are studying, look for and find any spiritual principles that apply to you and fellow believers in Christ. Every passage has them. Again, you may have to dig deep in some passages to find these gems. But the more you seek, the more God will meet you with His answers and His wisdom. (Biblica.com 2014)

Summary

In this chapter you learned how to process the meanings of what you have interpreted from

Scripture, so you can embed them into your spirit. You also learned how to apply them to your own life.

Coming Attractions

In the concluding chapter, if in a small group or classroom setting, you will discuss the results of your mini study. Additionally, you will be given tips on how to move forward on your own to continue what you have started during this course.

Points to Ponder

1. Compose a closing prayer asking God what He wants you to take away from this chapter. Then be still and listen. Write down whatever you think He is saying to you.

2. Perform a mini Bible study before next week using the first act from the article in Appendix F, *Help Reading the Bible*. This is a cumulative exercise, so use any of the things you have learned throughout all the chapters. If you are in a group, the members will discuss the results of the study during next week's meeting. If you are doing this on your own, find an advisor or mentor at your church to discuss your results with.

9

The Future Awaits

Next Steps

This chapter talks about ways to teach others what you know in a supportive way. Don't panic, this can be done anywhere; it does not need to be in a formal setting. Additionally, I have included recommended reading for the future.

Prayer

Father God, thank You for Your love and for Your instruction. Thank You for opening my spiritual eyes and ears throughout this study. I ask that You do it again as I work through this last chapter. Place in my heart what my next steps should be as I endeavor to walk the path You have set out for me. I ask this in Jesus' name, amen.

Chapter Verses: *Psalm 119:1-3; Titus 2:1*

ESV	*Psalm 119:1-3* [1]*Blessed are those whose way is blameless, who walk in the law of the LORD!* [2]*Blessed are those who keep his testimonies, who seek him with their whole heart,* [3]*who also do no wrong, but walk in his ways!* *Titus 2:1 But as for you, teach what accords with sound doctrine.*
CSB	*Psalm 119:1-3* [1]*How happy are those whose way is blameless, who walk according to the LORD's instruction!* [2]*Happy are those who keep his decrees and seek him with all their heart.* [3]*They do nothing wrong; they walk in his ways.* *Titus 2:1 But you are to proclaim things consistent with sound teaching.*
NIV	*Psalm 119:1-3* [1]*Blessed are those whose ways are blameless, who walk according to the law of the LORD.* [2]*Blessed are those who keep his statutes and seek him with all their heart—* [3]*they do no wrong but follow his ways.* *Titus 2:1 You, however, must teach what is appropriate to sound doctrine.*
NLT	*Psalm 119:1-3* [1]*Joyful are people of integrity, who follow the instructions of the LORD.* [2]*Joyful are those who obey his laws and search for him with all their hearts.* [3]*They do not compromise with evil, and they walk only in his paths.* *Titus 2:1 As for you, Titus, promote the kind of living that reflects wholesome teaching.*

There are two (2) chapter verses because they both are applicable to the future. Psalm 119:1-3 is a reminder that reading and studying the Bible is an ongoing process. If you are truly seeking God, you should be reading and studying the Bible on a regular basis. There is no other way to get to know Him. Titus 2:1 is a reminder that everyone is called to teach others. Your spiritual gift may not be teaching, but, as a Christian, you are called by God to share your knowledge of Christ with others.

First Your Mini Study

In chapter eight, you were instructed to do a small Bible study using Act 1 of the article in Appendix F. If you are part of a small group or a classroom setting, you and your fellow travelers will discuss the things you learned and the revelations you received from studying the passages. If you are going through these chapters on your own, find a trusted person or persons in your church to discuss your insights with. This person should be at least as far along in their walk with God as you are, preferably a little farther so he or she can give more in-depth guidance.

Now Your Future

Reading and studying the Bible, hopefully, will become a passion in your life that you cannot imagine living without. One way to do that is to keep in mind the positive things it does for you. For example, you could frequently complete this sentence, "Reading Scripture fills me with God the way ...." A couple of my responses have been, "... the warmth of the sun embraces me on a chilly day," or "... sitting and listening to a gentle brook babble over the rocks brings me peace." (Johnson 2003)

The point is, reinforce the good feelings you get from reading God's word with declarations of the satisfaction you get from it.

Spread the Word

Yes, this does mean that you should teach people about the Bible, but you should not go into panic mode at the thought. Consider this: you read something in the Bible that excites you, and you want to share what you discovered with someone. So, you find a friend, or even just an acquaintance, and share what God revealed to you through your reading. This person either gets excited at the new knowledge also, or he or she confirms your revelation. Either way, you have just taught part of the Bible.

The best way to retain something you have learned is to give it away, to teach it to someone else. By feeding someone else, you will feed your own heart and embed God's truths deeper into your spirit. (Grace to You 2015)

One avenue would be to find someone with a desire to learn more, but who knows less than you do, and pass on what you know. This can be done in a systematic way or as topics arise. Whatever scenario you use for sharing God's word, do it with humility. Knowledge makes a person arrogant, but love edifies (see Scripture #1). (Grace to You 2015)

Scripture 1: 1 Corinthians 8:1b, c

NIV; NLT	We know that "We all possess knowledge." But knowledge puffs up while love builds up.

Another way to get some practice with teaching the Bible in a safe environment is as part of a small group. Each person could study a different part of Scripture, or a different part of the lesson for that week, and then teach it to the rest of the group. After you have taught, gracefully consider the loving feedback that is provided by your fellow group members. Do not be defensive, which often is a person's first response to criticism. You might miss something that God wants you to know.

Recommended Reading

I highly recommend the following list of books as you continue in your quest to learn how to study the Bible more effectively. While you *can* read them in any order, I am suggesting the order in which they are listed. I believe it is the most logical for building your knowledge base and growing your spirit. All these books can be found on Amazon for less than $20.

4 KEYS TO HEARING GOD'S VOICE, Mark and Patti Virkler, 2010, Destiny Image Publishers, Inc. Shippensburg, PA. ISBN: 978-0-7684-3248.

Virkler's book changed my life. It taught me how to really hear God and how to have real conversations with Him. It has improved the quality of my Bible study immensely. But, more importantly, it has improved the quality of my relationship with God in every area of my life.

INTRODUCING THE BIBLE, 25th Anniversary Edition, William Barclay, 1972, revised & updated by John Rogerson, 1997. Abingdon Press, Nashville, TN. ISBN: 978-0-687-36590-6.

This is an excellent primer book for those just starting out. The information is presented in a way that is down-to-earth, and does not contain Bible-speak. It also appeals to those who have been reading and studying the Bible for a while but want to take it to a deeper level.

UNDERSTANDING THE BIBLE, Expanded Edition, John R. W. Stott, 1999. Zondervan, Grand Rapids, MI. ISBN: 0-310-41431-8.

Even though this was written decades after Barclay's *Introducing the Bible*, I found it very helpful in interpreting what I was reading by building on the knowledge acquired in the Barclay book. Again, the language is easy for the lay person to understand.

HOW TO READ THE BIBLE FOR ALL IT'S WORTH, 4th Edition, Gordon D. Fee and Douglas Stuart, 2014, Zondervan, Grand Rapids, MI. ISBN: 978-0-310-51782-5.

This book is for those who want to dig even deeper. It is hard core compared to the others. You will find within these pages the words *exegesis* and *hermeneutics*, as well as other more academic concepts. While it is harder to get through, it does lay out the nitty gritty of how to do it.

Personalize It

That's it. That's all I have for you on this topic. But God has much more. Now it is time for you to take the information you have been given, pray about it, and make your own plans.

IMMEDIATE PLANS

Take a moment and listen for what God wants you to do next. Just ask, "Lord, what should my next steps be?" and then be still and listen. Record the steps He gives you in your journal so you can refer back to them from time to time.

ONGOING PLANS

As you have seen, Bible reading is a life-long activity because, by design, you will never learn everything there is to know about God and the Bible until you see Jesus face-to-face. A good rule of thumb is to stop every now and then and take stock of what God has shown you over the past period of time. Here are some questions you could ask yourself: (ESV Study Bible 2011)

* What chunk of Scripture has made the most difference in my life?
* What verse or passage have I turned to most frequently?
* What makes these exact words frequently and immediately relevant?
* Have I taken the opportunity to share God's word with others?
* Is the process I am using still working for me, or do I need to make some adjustments?

In the business world there is a model for process implementation: plan ➔ execute ➔ evaluate ➔ adjust. Think of these questions as the *evaluate* part of the cycle. Let them inform you of areas that are or are not working so that you can *adjust* those that are not, i.e., make a new plan.

Remember, the process of studying the Bible is a fluid one. As you change, it will change. Periodic review of what you are doing, along with any changes you might want or need to implement, will help keep the process fresh and exciting.

Summary

This chapter contained a few words on teaching as well as suggestions on how to put God's Word into practice. Primarily, you were encouraged to take what you have learned throughout this guide and, using these suggestions, share God's Word with those in your community.

Coming Attractions

These are left up to you. My suggestion: Go forth and read … and re-read … and re-read … and re-read. Journal, journal, journal. God gives you deeper understanding the more you seek Him.

> A text may have a different significance or import for me each time I turn to it … for the Lord will speak to me where I am.
> —*Thelma Hall (Johnson 2003)*

Points to Ponder

I leave you with the prayer that all your journeys through the Bible will bless you, grow your spirit, and bring you into an increasingly deeper relationship with God the Father, God the Son, and God the Holy Spirit. May He grant you knowledge, discernment, and wisdom. May He show you the path He has planned for you and grant you His grace for your journey. I pray through my faith, by God's grace, and in the name of Jesus. Amen.

For your **final exercise**, compose a closing prayer asking God what He wants you to take away from this study. Then be still and listen. Write down whatever you think He is saying to you.

Appendix A: Web Addresses & Supplemental Resource List

This document lists all the URLs that are referenced in the study guide (websites and additional resources) and is provided so that, if you are using an electronic version, you do not have to type them in. (You might want to save this page to your own hard drive.)

To go to the web site, hold the CTRL key and click on the hyperlink. If that does not work, copy and paste the URL into the search box of your browser.

All the supplemental resources are available on the Google Drive. The URLs are listed in Table 2. However, some of these documents are provided in the appendices, also. Refer to Table 3 for the list of Appendices and their page numbers.

Table 1: URLs for Websites

CHAP #	WEB PAGE	URL
Intro, 4, 5	Blue Letter Bible	www.blueletterbible.org
1, 4, 5	YouVersion	www.bible.com
3	Translation Preference Survey	http://www.crosswalk.com/culture/infographics/quiz-which-bible-translation-should-you-choose.html
4	Crosswalk website	www.crosswalk.com
4	Bible Study Tools website	www.biblestudytools.com

Table 2: Documents on the Google Drive
NOTE: The files with an asterisk also appear in the Appendices. See Table 3 for page number.

CHAP   DOCUMENT: URL

Intro   **LEARNING STYLE INVENTORY:** https://docs.google.com/document/d/1MJE6hhst0xDrOexgzm6upyTf64Tj-PNlhzs3cpo_xLc/copy

Intro   ***URLS FOR WEBSITES & SUPPLEMENTAL RESOURCES:** https://drive.google.com/file/d/1f8nb23QuIH2_-pq_dzsW9y2YDK3p7KsA/copy

Intro   ***CHECK YOUR BIBLE IQ:** https://docs.google.com/document/d/1GYDZ0y8Ol0swWpNtVU4HSv8GwhCG6P3Fu9NsYhH08JE/copy

Intro   ***ANSWERS TO CHECK YOUR BIBLE IQ:** https://docs.google.com/document/d/16YLhj76Z2rJ7f3ImtKhIgEanNvA2OpZWF6OnA01dPZs/copy

Intro   **GROUP LEADERS GUIDE:** https://docs.google.com/document/d/1_3dJUSXehCenNQGkQ_-tAeRB0l32cWkG4aKePL9RV8/copy

Intro   **GETTING TO KNOW YOU-LEADER:** https://docs.google.com/document/d/1dE9gof36sOJZ7JDTCYlRgjWV02tWTVZOTAF_kpLQSW8/copy

Intro   **GETTING TO KNOW YOU-MEMBER:** https://docs.google.com/document/d/1Or5P8PkvzdJmZsEp-lIRylDF2L7q5U3yJIRrJcREY2M/copy

2   **MAPPING THE GOSPELS:** https://docs.google.com/document/d/1piXejx5jeYhc8e4ibyAuJaJVMV8L4j5CX0Qdn7rdGOI/copy

CHAP	DOCUMENT: URL
2,4,5	**NEW TESTAMENT IN A YEAR:** https://docs.google.com/spreadsheets/d/1IJA-Hgdw0nfvPZiWiEkovyOVgyAZflUqgsSvK7TZkM8/copy
2,4,5	**READ THE BIBLE CHRONOLOGICALLY:** https://docs.google.com/spreadsheets/d/19xdjeM614TiPxFa9cdypqEmfEDEmxYox-YtKToiC9A4/copy
2,4,5	**READ THE BIBLE OT & NT TOGETHER:** https://docs.google.com/spreadsheets/d/1cXNTv_X5hFAg_B3Hr-nkoLZC3ZZunUHpjn5609YM4VI/copy
3	**BIBLE TRANSLATION GUIDE (PDF):** https://drive.google.com/file//1JYvNV3yF1-uCGz0QWP2pA2R8qKQQ4_Px/view?usp=sharing
6	***JOURNAL MASTER: BIBLE READING:** https://docs.google.com/document/d/1r7G1PEhjEg5dSFTObdK8Krql186fdYdw56lh1tsvNnw/copy
6	***JOURNAL MASTER: TWO VERSES:** https://docs.google.com/document/d/1RuSXr6HsVCcVAHyxA_D_FEhNmtEpIEgKE7qk34WmgJE/copy
6	***JOURNAL MASTER: TWO-WAY JOURNALING:** https://docs.google.com/document/d/15v5eaODCDY1CMMLV58PZ8hCpH1o_LMJE2Z6omdb2I2Q/copy
6	***5 PROMPTS FOR JOURNALING THROUGH SCRIPTURE:** https://docs.google.com/document/d/1qS6PGVEh4DZHF4TS5ud1cTQ8MN-s7NS3aFWjYMN3WuE/copy
8	**VIRKLER-HOW TO MEDITATE ON SCRIPTURE:** https://docs.google.com/document/d/1tDzum5iU2yfUh61gdEzNG0Mx4o62kSgo4wtWAgzjvyM/copy
8	***PARABLE OF THE SOWER:** https://docs.google.com/document/d/1uC288USRC_47gRjnL3sASkuIvX0HqxQwROCgDcHIjN8/copy
8	***HELP READING THE BIBLE:** https://docs.google.com/document/d/1CuKNf0_VBQR0UxJx6ld-LzHC4NK5DQG_IIgykq9WoDU/copy
All	**LIST OF VERSES USED:** https://docs.google.com/document/d/18AL7k2zTYdax6FlSVU3VoPASJCK-e-a0NJsVfLlmDD8/copy

Table 3: Documents in the Appendices

APPENDIX	CONTENT	PAGE#
A	URLs for Referenced Websites and Supplemental Resource List	91
B	Check Your Bible IQ Quiz	93
C	Journaling Format Examples	97
D	5 Prompts for Journaling Through Scripture	103
E	Parable of the Sower	105
F	Help Reading the Bible	109
G	Answers to Bible IQ Quiz	113

Appendix B: Check Your Bible IQ

This quiz is taken verbatim from pages 4-5 of *The Complete Idiot's Guide to the Bible*. Take a moment to complete the quiz, then check the answers found in Appendix F. You may be surprised by how well you do on the quiz.

Circle the letter of the correct answer.

1. We got the word Bible from:

A. A variation of *Babylon*, which had extensive libraries.

B. The Hebrew word *biblius*, meaning "scroll that has no ending."

C. The Greek word *biblion*, meaning "roll" or "book."

D. An acronym for "**B**oy, **I**t's **B**ig, **L**eather, and **E**xpensive."

2. The original language(s) of the Bible are:

A. Hebrew, Greek, and Latin

B. Hebrew, Greek, and Aramaic

C. Hebrew, Latin, and Assyrian

D. 100 percent King James English

3. Which of the following are not books of the Bible?

A. Haggai and Philemon

B. Zephaniah and Zechariah

C. 2 Chronicles and 3 John

D. Guacamole and Minestrone

4. Canon refers to:

A. An overweight 1970s detective played by William Conrad.

B. Civil War weaponry.

C. A Greek word for a measuring device.

D. Writings that are accepted as authentic and inspired scripture.

5. The Apocrypha is:

A. A group of writings purported to be scripture but not accepted as such in every tradition.

B. A British term for drugstore.

C. A hill in Greece where the Parthenon was built.

D. A reference to the "four horsemen" in Revelations.

MATCH THE CORRECT NUMBERS TO THE APPROPRIATE STATEMENTS.

6. _____ Total number of books in the Bible.	1
7. _____ Number of Old Testament books.	2
8. _____ Number of New Testament books.	1,500
9. _____ Approximate number of Bible book authors.	27
10. _____ Period of years the Bible was written.	176
11. _____ Number of verses in the shortest chapter in the Bible.	39
12. _____ Number of verses in the longest chapter in the Bible.	66
13. The book with the most chapter divisions has _____ of them.	40
14. Of all the books ever written, the Bible is _____ of a kind.	150

See the next page for the last section of this quiz.

Finally, see if you can identify which of the following events are really found in the Bible and which are not.

For Real *No Way*

_____ _____ 15. After the flood, Noah gets drunk and naked.

_____ _____ 16. A guy named Balaam has an unsettling conversation with his talking donkey.

_____ _____ 17. A dead man touches Elisha's bones and comes back to life.

_____ _____ 18. Elijah calls down fire from heaven and then outruns a chariot down a mountain.

_____ _____ 19. Isaiah sees God on a throne surrounded by hovering, six-winged angels.

_____ _____ 20. Queen Jezebel is eaten by dogs.

_____ _____ 21. After surviving his big fish, a worm gets the better of Jonah.

_____ _____ 22. Uzzah touches the Ark of the Covenant and a year later his wife delivers septuplets.

_____ _____ 23. Wanting to prolong a victorious battle, Joshua commands the sun to stand still—and it does!

_____ _____ 24. God causes a shadow to move backward to prove the truth of Isaiah's message.

_____ _____ 25. In the course of a single night, Aaron's staff buds, blossoms, and produces almonds.

_____ _____ 26. Lot's daughters take turns getting him drunk and having sex with him so they can have children.

_____ _____ 27. King Herod takes credit for being a god and is struck down immediately and eaten by worms.

_____ _____ 28. After their sister is raped, some of Jacob's sons convince the family of the offender to be circumcised and then kill them while they are incapacitated.

_____ _____ 29. Moses spends so much time with God that his head begins to glow.

_____ _____ 30. King Solomon's famous wisdom fails him when he gets involved with 1,000 women.

_____ _____ 31. During the decline of Israel, things get so bad that people are reduced to eating donkey heads—and each other.

_____ _____ 32. Paul dies when bitten by a deadly viper, but comes back to life.

_____ _____ 33. A woman named Jael hammers the head of an enemy general to the ground with a tent peg.

_____ _____ 34. Jesus brings three dead people back to life.

_____ _____ 35. Paul and Barnabas are mistaken for the gods Zeus and Hermes.

Answers to this Bible quiz are found in Appendix G.

Appendix C: Journaling Format Samples

Journal Master → Bible Reading

day, Month, Year (i.e. Monday, January 1, 2021)

PASSAGE→ Enter Book, chapter(s) and verse(s) read.

STUDY: What do the notes in your study Bible say (if you have one)?

APPLICATION: What do the notes in your application Bible say (if you have one)?

SYNOPSIS: Write in your own words what you have read or understood from this passage. What is Scripture saying to you?

JOURNALING

Your prayer and asking God what he wants to say.

  Record God's response to you.

Your response to what God said. (These last two lines can be repeated if God responds to your response. It can develop into quite a conversation with Him.)

Your final prayer.

Journal Master → Two verses.
Day, Date (i.e. Monday, January 1, 2018)

Prayer

Type your opening prayer here. Or, if you are not into typing your prayer, use this as a prompt to remember to pray before you start.

From: (This is the date for the verse of the day and the devotional if it is different from today's date. I use this if I am trying to catch up and using verses from dates other than the current date.)

Verse of the Day (I use the one from YouVersion, but any source that provides a verse for each day will work. BLB has a couple of options.)

Reference (i.e. Mark 1:3)

ESV	*Note: these are the translations that I like. Use any translations that speak to you. Just use at least two of them.*
CSB	
NIV	
NLT	

Study (ESV): This is what my study Bible says about the verse(s).

Application (NIV): This is what the Life Application Bible says about the verse(s).

Devotional (Use any daily devotional that appeals to you. I use the ones written by Chris Tiegreen, but there are many excellent ones available.)

Reference

NLT*	
ESV	
CSB	
NIV	

Narrative

This section consists of excerpts from the narrative of the devotional.
Narrative Prayer (if there is one)

Bible Comments

Study (ESV):

Application (NIV):

Synthesis

Use this section to summarize and synthesize the information you gleaned from both sets of verses.

Journaling

This is my question to God.

God speaking—This is God's answer to me.

This is my response to God's answer. (These last two lines can be repeated if God responds to your response. It can develop into quite a conversation with Him.)

This is my final prayer.

Journal Master → Two-way Journaling

Date
Enter the current date.

Source
If the journaling was prompted by a particular item (i.e. a Bible passage or article) list it here. This helps your spiritual advisors understand where you are coming from and why you asked the question(s) you did.

Journaling
This is the spot for your opening prayer. Ask your question or questions here.

_____

Enter what you hear God say here.

The two text styles are not necessarily a requirement. I just find it easier to track the conversation.

_____

Enter your reaction to God's response here.

_____

These two sections can be repeated multiple times. If God's response prompts another question in your heart, feel free to ask it. Then record what He says. It can develop into quite a conversation with Him.

Be sure to end your last response with a closing prayer. I usually commit to doing whatever God said to do or repenting if He told me an area that needs work.

NOTE: Unlike the other formats, this one usually has a separate document for each session. (Although you can ask different questions in the same session.) If you choose to use this, you will want to save a master copy to start with each time, but don't forget to do a **SAVE AS** and give it a different name.

Creating separate documents facilitates sending them to your spiritual advisors, so that they do not have to scroll through many sessions to find the one you are asking about.

NOTE: The electronic copies of the sample versions for *Bible Reading* and *Two Verses* contained on the Google drive have a second page which has two purposes. First and foremost, it preserves all the styles used in the document so that you can set your style option to **IN USE**. Second, it provides an easy copy and paste option for creating subsequent entries in the journal.

Appendix D: 5 Prompts for Journaling Through Scripture

Find Comfort in Scripture
In these uncertain times, many of us are still reeling as we adjust to new realities, care for sick loved ones, grieve a loss, or battle weariness from a new work or home schedule. As Christians, our hope is in things unseen and we return again and again to the truth of Scripture, resting in its promises. As you spend time reading and journaling through the Bible, consider these five prompts to guide your study and reflection.

1. Be honest.
Be honest about how you are feeling. Highlight examples in the Psalms and books like Lamentations and Job where the writers aren't shy about telling God how they feel in their pain, confusion, exhaustion, and frustration (see Job 3:23-26). Biblical writers were often transparent and forthright with both their joys and hardships; we should be, too. Write out your honest thoughts alongside similar passages.

2. Learn about God's heart toward those who suffer.
Read through the psalms of lament. How does the psalmist respond to God's faithfulness (see Psalm 103)? Read through large portions of books like Jeremiah and Job. How do the books end? What hope do they offer to those in Christ? Spend some time writing out ways that these stories give us hope in our own uncertain times.

3. Pray hopefully.
Use Scripture to pray for those who are hurting, sick, and lonely. Journal and pray through verses that speak to God's protection of the weak, the unshakeable hope we have in Christ, and the defeat of death because of Christ's resurrection (see Matthew 24:35).

4. Focus on what is unchanging.
Reflect on what is unchanging about who God is when circumstances are shifting. Do a character study on the attributes of God. Go to Scripture to meditate on how he is *unlike* us—and why that is ultimately good news for us as finite beings (see Isaiah 55:8-9).

5. End with gratitude.
Read through passages that remind you of the rich mercy believers enjoy because of Christ. Record lists of the good gifts in your life and pray to embrace them fully—not just for their sake, but so they might ultimately point you back to the Lord (see James 1:17).

Use this page for notes.

Appendix E: Parable of the Sower

Matthew 13:3-9 (Parable)

³Then he told them many things in parables, saying: "Consider the sower who went out to sow. ⁴"As he sowed, some seed fell along the path, and the birds came and devoured them. ⁵Other seed fell on rocky ground where it didn't have much soil, and it grew up quickly since the soil wasn't deep. ⁶But when the sun came up, it was scorched, and since it had no root, it withered away. ⁷Other seed fell among thorns, and the thorns came up and choked it. ⁸Still other seed fell on good ground and produced fruit: some a hundred, some sixty, and some thirty times what was sown. ⁹Let anyone who has ears listen." **(CSB)**

Matthew 13:18-23 (Explanation of Parable)

¹⁸"So listen to the parable of the sower: ¹⁹When anyone hears the word about the kingdom and doesn't understand it, the evil one comes and snatches away what was sown in his heart. This is the one sown along the path. ²⁰And the one sown on rocky ground—this is one who hears the word and immediately receives it with joy. ²¹But he has no root and is short-lived. When distress or persecution comes because of the word, immediately he falls away. ²²Now the one sown among the thorns—this is one who hears the word, but the worries of this age and the deceitfulness of wealth choke the word, and it becomes unfruitful. ²³But the one sown on the good ground—this is one who hears and understands the word, who does produce fruit and yields: some a hundred, some sixty, some thirty times what was sown." **(CSB)**

Synopsis

HARD PATH:	Birds snatch away—Person does not understand the Word; therefore, does not receive the Word.
ROCKY PLACES:	Sprang up quickly, sun burned out—Person understands and receives the Word, but does not change behavior.
AMONG THORNS:	Plants grew, weeds choked out—Person understands and receives the Word, starts out changing behavior, but worries of life and deceitfulness take over and reverts to old ways.
GOOD SOIL:	Produces fruit—Person understands, receives, and applies the Word. Lives a life focused on God, does not revert to old ways.

USE OF PARABLES
- Compares something familiar to something unfamiliar.
- Compels listeners to discover truth, while concealing truth from those who are too lazy or stubborn to see it.
- If you are honestly searching, the truth becomes clear.
- Beware: don't force parables (or any Scripture) to say what you *want* them to say.

NOTES ABOUT THIS PARABLE (TAKEN FROM LIFE APPLICATION BIBLE)
- Belief cannot be forced. It is a miracle of God's Holy Spirit as He uses the words of teachers, preachers, and witnesses to lead others to Him.
- Human ears hear many sounds; it takes a deeper kind of listening (spiritual ears) to hear God's truth. The four types of soil represent different responses to God's message. People respond differently because they are in different states of readiness.

- While the second and third types of soil show belief for a short while, only the fourth soil type remains consistent in God's worth and shows fruit.
- What kind of soil are you?
- You can change your soil through seeking and studying.

Appendix F: Help Reading the Bible

How do you read the Bible? As a reference book? An instruction manual? A story? At its core, the Bible is a drama, the story of God rescuing and redeeming the world. It's a diverse collection of books, but the same story runs throughout, from Genesis to Revelation. Get a sweeping view of the Bible's story by following our *Drama of the Bible* reading plan.

NOTE: This reading plan is also available in some of our NIV paperback Bibles. Published Wednesday, January 15, 2014. http://www.biblica.com/en-us/bible/help-reading-the-bible/ Downloaded 8/14/2015

The Drama of the Bible: A Six-Act Reading Plan
To understand the Bible, you must get to know its characters, understand its setting, and follow its plot. That's because the Bible is a story—the truest, most important story ever told. It is the real saga of a particular people, how God called them and used them to bring blessing to all people.

The individual parts of the Bible will only make sense if you know the bigger story. The climax of the story—the death and resurrection of Jesus—only makes sense once you've followed the earlier parts as a story, once you've felt the tension and wrestled with its major conflict.

Below is a Bible reading plan that highlights the drama of Scripture in five key acts. In two months or less, you can get a *big picture* view of the biblical story, a foundation that will stay with you for a lifetime.

Act 1: God's Intention
Day 1: Creation (Genesis 1; 2:1-3)
Day 2: Praise God for his creation (Psalm 8)
Day 3: Praise to the Creator of all things (Psalm 104)
Day 4: Praise for creating me (Psalm 139)

Act 2: Exile
Day 5: The fall into sin (Genesis 3)
Day 6: Noah, the flood and the ark (Genesis 6, 7, 8, 9:1-17)
Day 7: A prayer of repentance (Psalm 51)
Day 8: No one is righteous (Romans 3:9-26)

Act 3: Calling Israel to a Mission
Day 9: God's covenant with Abraham (Genesis 12:1-9, 15:1-21)
Day 10: Abraham almost sacrifices his son Isaac (Genesis 22:1-19)
Day 11: Jacob receives his father's blessing (Genesis 27:1-40)
Day 12: Jacob's (Israel's) family (Genesis 29:16-35, 30:1-24)
Day 13: Joseph the dreamer (Genesis 37:2-36; see also chapters 39-50)
Day 14: Moses is born in Egypt (Exodus 1; 2:1-10)
Day 15: Ten plagues (Exodus 7:14-24; 8; 9; 10; 11:1-10)
Day 16: The Passover (Exodus 12:1-17)
Day 17: The Israelites leave Egypt (Exodus 12:17-50; 13; 14; 15:1-21)
Day 18: God's covenant with Israel (Exodus 19; 20)
Day 19: Rahab the prostitute hides the Israelite spies (Joshua 2)
Day 20: God keeps his promise (Joshua 23; 24)
Day 21: David kills Goliath (1 Samuel 17)

Day 22: David becomes king (2 Samuel 5:1-5)
Day 23: God's promise to David (2 Samuel 7)
Day 24: David and Bathsheba (2 Samuel 11; 12:1-25)
Day 25: The Lord is my shepherd (Psalm 23)
Day 26: A prayer of thanksgiving (Psalm 100)
Day 27: Israel sent into exile (2 Chronicles 36:15-23)
Day 28: Queen Esther saves her people (Esther 1)
Day 29: Messiah's birth prophesied (Isaiah 9:1-7)
Day 30: God's promise to return (Isaiah 52:1-12)
Day 31: Daniel's dream of God's kingdom (Daniel 7)

Act 4: The Surprising Victory of Jesus

Day 32: The birth of Jesus (Luke 1-2)
Day 33: The temptation of Jesus (Matthew 4:1-11; Luke 4:1-13)
Day 34: The Sermon on the Mount (Matthew 5; 6)
Day 35: Jesus shares his calling with the people (Luke 4:16-30)
Day 36: Jesus' teaching on prayer (Luke 11:1-13)
Day 37: The lost son (Luke 15)
Day 38: New birth (John 3)
Day 39: Jesus is the resurrection and the life (John 11)
Day 40: Three prayers of Jesus (John 17)
Day 41: The Lord's Supper (Luke 22:7-38; 1 Corinthians 11:17-34)
Day 42: The death of Jesus (Luke 23:26-56; John 19:16-42)
Day 43: The resurrection of Jesus (Luke 24; John 20)
Day 44: Jesus ascends into heaven (Acts 1:1-11)

Act 5: The Renewed People of God

Day 45: The Great Commission from Jesus (Matthew 28:16-20)
Day 46: The coming of the Holy Spirit (Acts 2:1-21)
Day 47: "Repent and be baptized" (Acts 2:22-47)
Day 48: Jesus, the fulfillment of Abraham's covenant (Acts 3)
Day 49: Salvation in Jesus alone (Acts 4)
Day 50: Paul's conversion (Acts 9:1-31)
Day 51: Paul's testimony before King Agrippa (Acts 25:23-27; 26:1-32)
Day 52: What real love is (1 Corinthians 13)
Day 53: The fruit of the Holy Spirit (Galatians 5:22-23)
Day 54: The armor of God (Ephesians 6:10-18)
Day 55: Imitating Christ (Philippians 2:1-11)
Day 56: Heroes of the faith (Hebrews 11)
Day 57: Faith in action (James 2:14-26)

Act 6: God Comes Home

Day 58: The return of Christ (1 Thessalonians 4:13-18; 2 Peter 3:3-14)
Day 59: The new heaven and earth (Revelation 21-22)

Appendix G: Answers to Bible Quiz

These are the answers to the Bible quiz found in Appendix A.

1. C.

2. B—Aramaic was probably the colloquial language of Palestine and the primary language of Jesus. It was used occasionally in both the Old and New Testaments.

3. D.

4. C and D

5. A—The other responses refer to *apothecary*, *Acropolis*, and *apocalypse*.

6. 66

7. 39

8. 27

9. 40

10. 1,500

11. 2

12. 176

13. 150

14. 1

15-35. The events described in #22 and #32 have been altered, so they are untrue. But all the others are found in the Bible [and are true].

Use this page for notes.

Works Cited

Advanced Training Institute International. 2015. "What Is Rhema?" in *Scripture for Personal Application* (blog). Accessed May 17, 2015, https://atii.org/what-is-a-rhema/.

Barclay, William, (1972) 1997. *Introducing the Bible*, 25th Anniversary ed. Edited by John Rogerson. Nashville, TN: Abingdon Press.

Bell, James, S. Jr., and Stan Campbell. 2003. *Complete Idiot's Guide to the Bible*, 2nd ed. United States: Alpha.

Biblica.com. 2014. *Help Reading the Bible*. Accessed August 8, 2015, http://www.biblica.com/en-us/bible/help-reading-the-bible/.

Butler, Trent C., Gen. ed. 2003. *Holman's Illustrated Bible Dictionary*, revised ed. Nashville, TN: Holman Reference.

Crossway. 2020. *5 Prompts for Studying the Bible*. Accessed April 30, 2020. https://www.crossway.org/articles/5-prompts-for-journaling-through-scripture/?utm_source=Crossway+Marketing&utm_campaign=9f6f922e99-20200429+-+General+-+Journaling+Scripture&utm_medium=email&utm_term=0_0275bcaa4b-9f6f922e99-296651201

Dekker, Ted. 2016. *The Creative Way: A Course in Transformational Fiction*. USA: Outlaw Studios.

ESV Study Bible. 2011. Wheaton, IL: Crossway

Fairchild, Mary. 2015a. "How to Do Daily Devotions." *ThoughtCo* (website). Accessed February 28, 2018, https://www.thoughtco.com/how-to-do-daily-devotions-701262.

Fairchild, Mary. 2015b. "Learn an Easy Step-By-Step Method of Studying the Bible." *ThoughtCo* (website). Accessed August 21, 2015, https://www.thoughtco.com/how-to-study-the-bible-700238#step-heading.

Fee, Gordon D. and Douglas Stuart. 2014. *How to Read the Bible for All Its Worth*, 4th ed. Grand Rapids, MI: Zondervan.

Grace to You. 2015. *How to Study Your Bible*. Accessed August 14, 2015, http://www.gty.org.

Johnson, Jan. 2003. "Study & Meditation." In *Spiritual Disciplines Bible Studies*, 177-150. Downers Grove, IL: Intervarsity Press.

Kohlenberger, John R., ed. 2015. *The NIV Exhaustive Bible Concordance*, 3rd ed. Grand Rapids, MI: Zondervan.

Life Application Study Bible (NIV), 2011. Grand Rapids, MI: Zondervan.

Merriam-Webster's Collegiate Dictionary, 2014. 11th ed. Springfield, MA: Merriam-Webster, Inc.

Meyer, Joyce. 2015. *How to Study the Bible*. Accessed February 28, 2018, https://joycemeyer.org/everydayanswers/ea-teachings/how-to-study-the-bible.

Radiant Church. 2015. *Pathways to Kingdom Living*. Kalamazoo, MI: self-published.

Stott, John R. W. 1999. *Understanding the Bible*, expanded ed. Grand Rapids, MI: Zondervan.

Stott, John R. W. 2008. *Basic Christianity*, 3rd ed. Grand Rapids, MI: William B. Eerdmans Publishing.

Strong, James. 1979. *Strong's Exhaustive Concordance of the Bible*. Nashville, TN: Thomas Nelson Publishers.

Virkler, Mark, and Patti Virkler. 2013. "A 7 Step Mediation Process Explored." *Communion With God Ministries*. Accessed June 27, 2017, www.cwgministries.org/meditation.

Wellman, Jack. 2015. "5 Tips for Picking the Best Bible Translation." *What Christians Want to Know* (website). Accessed May 21, 2015, http://www.whatchristianswanttoknow.com/five-tips-for-picking-the-best-bible-translation/.

Printed in the United States
by Baker & Taylor Publisher Services